The CALM CATALYSTS

HOW SILENT LEADERS DRIVE BOLD WINS

BRAHMANAND SAVANTH

Clever Fox® PUBLISHING
Chennai • Bangalore

CLEVER FOX PUBLISHING
Chennai, India

Published by CLEVER FOX PUBLISHING 2025

ISBN: 978-93-6707-481-7

TABLE OF CONTENTS

PREFACE

Leadership is not about who holds the microphone. It is about who shifts the wave before anyone notices the current has changed. Over two decades in the world of technology, strategy, and leadership, I recognize from self-reflection, The real transformation in organizations does not always shout from the rooftops — it quietly begins in mindsets, values, and everyday behaviours.

"The Calm Catalysts" was born from that realization.

This book is not about celebrated CEOs or grand visions declared from stages. It is about the quiet influences—the people, principles, and patterns—that drive organizations steadily, silently, and surely toward success. These are the fine distinctions, the middle managers who hold the cultural threads together, the values not much talked about, but everyone feels, the habits that shape outcomes more than any dashboard ever could.

In the initial years of my career, I had the privilege of drawing inspiration from one of the most revolutionary thinkers in corporate leadership—Vineet Nayar, the former CEO of HCL Technologies. His philosophy, *"Employees First, Customers Second,"* was not just a catchy mantra. It was a great shift in how organizations viewed people, purpose, and power. It left a permanent mark on me. His belief that trust, transparency, and empowerment—not control—unlock performance, reshaped my understanding of what leadership could truly be.

Much of what I internalized from his philosophy found its way into my own leadership style—not in imitation, but as an inspiration. Just as Vineet held up a mirror to traditional leadership and asked it to change, I hope this book holds up a quiet torch in the noisy corridors of business.

As I moved through roles, led global teams, mentored aspirants, and led critical transitions, I began to observe these invisible forces at play—forces that made the difference between surviving and celebrating. This book is my attempt to give voice to those forces. Make visible what has long remained unspoken. Offer a lens through which both aspiring professionals and seasoned leaders can view their environments more consciously and perhaps lead with deeper clarity and impact.

Each chapter reflects a blend of lived experience, reflection, and practical insight. You'll find stories, metaphors, and questions—because change does not begin with answers, it begins with awareness.

If this book moves you to listen more deeply to your people, to question the invisible habits that shape your culture, and to lead with presence instead of pressure, then it has served its purpose. And if, along the way, it inspires even one reader the way Vineet's philosophy inspired me, I will consider it a quiet victory.

To all "The Calm Catalysts" out there who remain unspoken—you have always mattered. This is your mirror.

Brahmanand Savanth
June 2025

PART I

THE UNSEEN BLUEPRINT

CHAPTER 1

THE SILENT HARMONY — EMOTIONAL ENERGY AT WORK

1.1 Emotions as performance multipliers

Now, if you ever find yourself walking through the fine and beautiful city of Bangalore—a place where buildings rise faster than bread in a hot oven—you might come across a certain glass office standing way up high, standing tall like a statement in glass and steel. This was the world of Vedika, a manager so organised, you would think she ironed her calendar before hanging it on the wall.

Vedika ran her days like a steam engine on polished rails. Her inbox was emptier than a church on Saturday night, her to-do list split into fancy quadrants that would make a general blush, she wore crisp cotton kurtas, and her tea came by the hour like clockwork soldiers—green at morning, tulsi at noon. She did not walk so much, and her shoes knew better than to disturb the silence with any sort of clicking or clacking.

Folks around the office looked up to her, sure they did. She was reliable, like the morning sun or a mother-in-law's advice—always there, never late, but not always warm. Her glass cabin sat high on the 21st floor, catching just enough sunlight to remind folks what ambition looked like. It smelled of lemongrass and caution. Clean, neat, and just a tad too quiet—like a museum where no one really knows what they're looking at.

Now, on paper, her team was humming along—deadlines met, reports filed, and clients patted on the head like good dogs. But down below, under that shiny surface, the engine was losing steam. The fire had gone cold.

Once upon a time, that office was alive with laughter, debates over chai, and big wild ideas scrawled on post-it notes like treasure maps. But now? Well, it had all gone quiet. The kind of quiet that does not bring peace—it brings distance. Smiles were painted on, like fresh coats of paint on old wood. Nobody argued. Nobody dared to spark. And where ideas once bounced around like firecrackers in a tin can, now they just sat there, fretting like teenagers at a family dinner.

Folks showed up, did their job, and went home. They followed the rules but left their hearts at the door. And let me tell you, when work becomes just a trade of time for money, instead of a spark for the soul—that is when you know something mighty important has gone missing.

Well now, it was on one of those regular old Mondays—the kind that sneak up on you like a pickpocket in a busy market, Vedika first noticed the air had turned boring in her little kingdom of order. The stand-up meeting, which used to crackle with voices and half-baked ideas, felt more like a lecture read by tired spirits.

Raavi, the energetic designer with fire in her fingers and mischief in her mind, spoke in flat tones like she had swallowed a ruler. Did not even mention the clever little trick she had pulled off over the weekend, the one that could have saved the UX team a week's worth of headaches. And Abhay, the tech lead who once made even debugging sound like poetry on a bicycle ride, well—he talked like he was reading an obituary. His own. Nobody cracked a joke. Nobody cut in. The room sat heavy with silence, like fog in a valley.

Now Vedika, being a woman of logic, chalked it up to plain old fatigue. Targets had been running them hard, like a donkey cart down a dusty road in summer. So, she tried to oil the wheels—moved some timelines, trimmed meetings, even threw in a few cheery quotes in the newsletter. Something about eagles soaring and dreams waking before dawn. But no matter how many feathers she fluffed, the bird refused to sing.

Then came a project delay.

Now, it was not a major landslide—just a missed milestone. But what knocked the wind out of her was not the delay itself—it was the way her team took it. Like passengers watching a train move past they never intended to catch. No rush to course correct. No storm of ideas or late-night pizza plans. Just a sort of quiet surrender. As if success and failure had both dissolved into echoes—something to ignore like ceiling fans or office air fresheners.

One morning with rain gods in mood to wash the city clean, with the monsoon clouds moping above the skyline and the windows weeping gentle drops, Vedika stood at the glass like a woman trying to read the world's mood. A bird sang somewhere in the wet trees. The wind danced in the lawn, free as children let out of school. And for the first time in a long time, Vedika's mind drifted away from charts and calendars.

She started wondering..

When did her team stop laughing?

When did eyes stop shining with mischief, with that wild itch to break something just to make it better?

When did folks start pushing away their real thoughts like smuggled truth behind polite silence?

And more importantly, when did *we* stop feeling alive at work?

A memory sneaked in, quiet as a stray pup during dinnertime. Two years back, she had walked into that same team—not as captain, but as a team member. The place was a beautiful mess back then. Loud. Unruly. Alive. Ideas spilled onto whiteboards like gravy on a steel plate. People argued with the heat of chili but the warmth of trust. Lunch breaks were rituals, not meetings with snacks. She remembered Raavi bringing hot Pakoras on a rainy day—the whole floor smelling like happiness. And Abhay, fixing bugs while spinning verses about karma and code, like a digital poet with a keyboard for a sitar.

Now everything was... clean. Orderly. Predictable. Like her desk.

That day, Vedika walked the office floor slowly, like a stranger observing a museum of memories. Desks were lined with screens, heads bent low, ear buds in. A team of twenty-three people, all connected by VPNs but disconnected by energy. She paused by one desk—a new intern, Ishaan, who had joined three weeks ago. He looked up at her, startled, eyes wary.

"How are you settling in?" she asked.

"All good," he said too quickly.

She noticed his workspace. No photos. No mementoes. Just a borrowed laptop and a bottle of water. Not even a Post-it. It struck her—nobody was leaving traces of themselves anymore. They were showing up, but not arriving. Occupying chairs, but not space.

That night, she stayed back late. She opened old team folders, clicked through archived Zoom recordings. In one from last year, there was laughter. Someone spilled coffee. Abhay teased Raavi about her obsession with gradients. There was background noise—not of machines, but of belonging.

And in another, more recent clip—silence. Clean updates. Muted reactions.

What had changed?

She had.

Vedika realized that in her pursuit of precision, she had drained the workplace of its pulse. She had become a leader who optimized output but forgot to nourish the soul. Her tone, her structure, her very presence had discouraged vulnerability. People no longer felt safe to speak freely. She had mistaken control for care.

Outside, the rain tapped louder.

That night, Vedika did not drive home immediately. She walked into the cafeteria, now dark, and sat by the vending machine. The aroma of stale coffee hung in the air. She took out her phone and typed a message on the team group:

"Tomorrow, bring a story. Not a work one. Any story. Something that moved you. We'll begin the day with stories."

She hit send.

The message got two read ticks. No reply.

Still, she felt lighter.

The next morning, the conference room was filled with awkward energy. People shuffled in, uncertain. Raavi clutched her phone, unsure. Abhay sat at the back. Ishaan looked terrified.

Vedika began.

She told them a story from her college days—of a debate she lost, but how the opponent had become her best friend. Of how failure felt then: raw, personal, and alive. She laughed at herself. It was a small laugh, but it echoed.

Then Raavi spoke. She shared a childhood memory of making a kite with her grandfather.

Abhay talked about his dog.

One by one, people unzipped their shells.

By 11 a.m., nothing had changed on the dashboard. But the air? It was different. There was warmth. Curiosity. Someone even asked, "Can we do this every week?"

Vedika smiled. She did not reply. But inside, she knew: the team had not stopped being alive. They had only forgotten what it felt like. And perhaps, so had she.

That day, no great decision was made. No budget was reallocated. But something shifted. The invisible engine that powers every workplace—emotion—had been restarted.

And as the day unfolded, stories kept trickling in like water from forgotten wells. Each tale added a drop of liveliness. And Vedika, for the first time in months, felt something to cheer in the room—a collective heartbeat.

It was not productivity, nor was it process. It was the presence.

Somewhere between the coffee spills and coding poetry, a truth had sneaked in: ***You do not build great teams by enforcing silence. You build them by inviting voices*.**

And maybe, just maybe, the next breakthrough would not come from a strategy document—but from a story shared over tea.

A Murmur Below the Noise

Now, it is a peculiar thing about battles, whether fought with swords or spreadsheets—it is not always the loudest fellow on the field who wins. Mostly, it is the quiet one. The one who listens close—not to orders, but to the hush in a crowded room, the vibration in a handshake, the way a land breathes when no one is looking. You see, a true leader does not march to the beat of targets or deadlines. They move to the music below it all—the kind you feel in your chest before you ever hear it with your ears.

In the modern-day battlefield we call the workplace, there is a curious sort of energy that is not found in quarterly charts or daily stand-ups. It is called **emotional energy**, and though it does not show up in reports, it will make or break a team quicker than any missed metric. When it flows, people come alive. Ideas bloom, jokes fly, and people stay after meetings just to chat. And when it dries up? Well, even the best-laid plans dry up like enthusiasm in a Monday meeting.

Take Vedika, for instance. Smart girl. Well-organized, Sharp. Ran her meetings like clockwork—every word in place, every chart upright. But something was missing. Her folks were not stumbling… they were fading. Drifting. She did not ask how they were doing "really doing?". Did not hear the tired breath behind a "fine," or see the weight behind a smile that did not quite reach the eyes.

What Vedika had not reckoned with was that emotional energies do not shout—it *whispers.* And if you are not tuned to listen, you'll miss the moment it leaves. It is in the pause before someone speaks up. In the way they nod, more polite than present. It is in the silence that settles when trust walks out the door.

Every gesture—every glance, word, shrug, or sigh—adds or subtracts from the team's invisible bank. And if you keep making withdrawals without making deposits, well, you're headed for bankruptcy of a different kind. Not one you will see in red ink—but in empty stares and early logoffs.

Then one day, Vedika started to notice. The little things. The headphones Raavi wore to lunch. The birthday board gathering dust. Abhay's precise 6:00 p.m. sign-off, like clockwork. These weren't coincidences—they were signs. Flags waving not for attention, but for connection.

That is when it struck her: being a leader is not about pushing people harder—it is about managing to their spirit. Like any good farmer knows, you do not pull on crops to make them grow. You nurture the soil. Water it. Let the sun do its job. And most of all, you *notice.*

So, she began asking the right questions. Not in surveys, but over chai. Not in checkboxes, but in curious, open pauses.

And little by little, things changed.

The intern picked up sketching again. Raavi put up fairy lights. Abhay cracked a joke—first time in months. Nothing big. But impactful in a positive way.

Because the soul of a workplace is not in the speeches or dashboards. It is in those small, invisible gestures that whisper: *"I see you."*

It is the nod that says, *"You belong."*

And if you ask me, that is the real engine behind any successful team. The Unspoken calm catalyst we forget too often—but remember just in time.

The Science That the Village Elder Knew

Long before neuroscientists spoke of the amygdala and cortisol, our elders knew: "A word can heal, a tone can wound." What modern labs now confirm, village wisdom always sensed—that emotions decide long before logic explains.

Today, neuroscience maps our emotional responses to the limbic system, where the amygdala acts like a watchdog, scanning every interaction for signs of danger or connection. When we experience stress—say, a manager's cold tone or criticism—our brain floods our system with cortisol. This stress hormone sharpens our fight-or-flight instincts but dulls our creativity and collaboration. On the other hand, oxytocin—the so-called 'bonding hormone'—is released during moments of trust, empathy, and shared joy, promoting openness and innovation.

In every meeting, every conversation, every hallway glance, our brains are constantly evaluating one core question: Am I safe?

Not just physically—but emotionally, socially, psychologically.

A kind smile can trigger oxytocin, unlocking imagination and inviting risk-taking. A dismissive silence can activate the amygdala, shutting down exploration and triggering conformity. Emotional energy is like the monsoon wind—you cannot see it, but you can feel its effect in every branch it touches. It carries the power to nourish or wither.

In evolutionary terms, this sensitivity to emotional cues was once essential for survival in tribes. In workplaces, it remains essential—but for belonging, not survival. Our predecessors huddled for warmth and safety. Today, teams huddle for trust and synergy. When psychological safety is absent, people play small. They avoid disagreement, camouflage their creativity, and guard their inner world. But when safety is present, they contribute not just their hands, but their hearts.

The logic of emotion is not irrational—it is simply older. Deeper. More fundamental. Before the neocortex can draft a response, our bodies and hearts have already voted.

The future of great leadership will likely transcend traditional competencies like strategic vision and digital proficiency, shifting instead toward a more nuanced, human-centered skill—emotional literacy. With rapid technological advancement, the leaders who stand out will be those who can read a room with precision, detecting unspoken tensions, hidden fatigue, or silent enthusiasm. They will listen not just to what is said, but to what remains unspoken, asking the right questions to uncover deeper concerns and motivations. This ability to navigate the emotional undercurrents of a team will be just as critical as optimizing workflows or leveraging AI.

The next generation of leaders will need to operate on two levels: the analytical, where data and efficiency drive decisions, and the emotional, where empathy and connection build trust. They will balance hard skills with soft power, recognizing that sustainable success depends not just on productivity, but on psychological safety and engagement. When automation handles routine tasks, the irreplaceable value of leadership will lie in understanding people—anticipating their needs, inspiring their potential, and cultivating authentic relationships.

Ultimately, emotional literacy may become the defining differentiator between good and extraordinary leadership. The leaders who master this skill will not only drive performance but also create workplaces where individuals feel valued, leading to higher collaboration, innovation, and resilience in the face of change.

Because under the KPIs and dashboards, or the revenue graphs and sprint charts, lies the truest metric of all:

Does your workplace feel alive?

And if it does not, it is time to stop looking at numbers—and start listening to the silence.

As the Alan Walker song Alone says, *"We all need that someone who gets you like no one else."* This is not just a lyric—it is the truth that echoes through every workplace. In the buzz of deadlines and dashboards, what we quietly crave is emotional resonance:

someone who understands the silences as much as their words. In thriving teams, that "someone" does not always wear a title. Often, it is these catalysts—the empathetic peers, the middle managers who listen more than they speak, the quiet supporters who nudges us forward. When emotional energy flows freely, connection becomes the real productivity driver.

1.2 The Quiet Turnaround

It was an old janitor, Bala, who unknowingly showed Vedika the way. Every morning, as he swept the corridors of the tech park humming an old folk tune, he would greet each person with a question that did not quite fit the modern pace of life: "You seem cheerful today!!, and Nice to see you cheerful today" Not the routine, "How are you?" that most leaders were conditioned to ask. But something much deeper. Something that sought not just a status update, but a human connection.

At first, Vedika barely noticed Bala's morning ritual. She was preoccupied with turnarounds, restructuring, and managing the toxic after-effects of a merger that had left teams disoriented. Her office buzzed with stress, and her inbox was a battlefield of fire fights. But over time, a subtle awareness took root. She began to *observe* Bala.

Each morning, he moved with time and sparkle, like someone who was not rushing against time but flowing with it. His broom touched not just the dust on the floor but the hearts of the people walking by. And the people responded. Even those usually absorbed in their headphones stopped, smiled, and replied. Some lingered. Some laughed. Some unburdened.

And in that moment, she realized. *Leadership was not about control. It was about connection.*

For Vedika, this realization did not descend like a thunderclap. It unfolded gradually, like a sunrise. Bala, a man with no title, no authority, and no KPI to measure impact, had become the cultural heart of the office.

The Turning Point

Vedika, an MBA graduate from a top institute, had always led from the front—decisive, driven, and delivery-oriented. She could break down complex problems, design frameworks, and align metrics like a pro. But this moment humbled her. What Bala did was leadership of another kind—*leadership from the soul.*

She remembered what Shiv Khera once said in *You Can Win*: "Winners don't do different things, they do things differently."

So, Vedika decided to do things differently. Not by rewriting strategies or hiring consultants, but by shifting the emotional temperature of the workplace.

The Shift

The first change came in the Monday meetings. Instead of launching into agenda items, Vedika began with a deceptively simple question:

"What gave you energy this week at work?"

At first, there was silence. People shifted in their chairs. But slowly, the answers came. Someone spoke about the support he got from a peer while working on a project plan, someone said the confidence with which a call they completed with a cranky customer, and some even shared personal ones like their child's drawing. Another about a late-night coding breakthrough. Someone else is about to finally plant that herb garden.

That small tweak turned transactional meetings into moments of trust.

She celebrated not just quarterly numbers but *kindness*. When Anjali stayed late to help a colleague debug code, Vedika made sure the story was shared. When Naveen paused his vacation to help close a ticket, she appreciated the *spirit*, not just the outcome.

Every Friday, Vedika closed the week with a five-minute ritual:

"Let's appreciate one colleague who made your week easier or better."

No HR tool, no surveys, no jargon. Just genuine recognition.

The Ripple Effect

Slowly, like grass after rain, the energy returned. The team laughed more. People stayed after meetings to chat. Whiteboards filled up again—not with deadlines, but ideas.

And the best part? The client, unaware of these cultural changes, remarked on a call:

"Something feels different. You all sound more alive."

That was Vedika's moment of quiet victory. Because leadership is not always about raising the bottom line. Sometimes, it is about lifting the *human spirit.*

Leadership Learnings:

1. **Titles don't lead. People do.** Bala, the janitor, was not part of any leadership committee. But he influenced culture more deeply than many with corner offices. Leadership begins with *intent,* not designation.
2. **Connect before you correct.** Vedika realized that genuine connection builds the trust required for meaningful feedback. A team that feels seen, heard, and valued responds better to change.
3. **Leadership is a transfer of belief.** When Vedika asked, "What gave you energy?" she shifted focus from gaps to growth, from flaws to feelings. People rose to the level of belief she invested in them.
4. **Small actions create a big impact.** Recognition, empathy, and curiosity cost nothing but pay priceless dividends. Culture does not change through PowerPoints. It changes through presence.
5. **Emotions are data, too.** Bala's simple greeting was emotional intelligence in action. He intuitively asked the right question—one that cut through hierarchy, stress, and silence.

1.3 The Greater Realization

Vedika began to see her team not as resources, but as *resonances* of human potential. She coached her managers to look beyond performance sheets and see the person behind the role. She built emotional literacy into leadership reviews.

When a team member went through a personal loss, she arranged backup without fanfare. When someone cracked a big client deal, she celebrated with their family.

The Vedika who once obsessed over dashboards had now found wisdom in doorways.

Summing Up:

At the end of the quarter, as she reflected on the journey, Vedika realized: she had not changed the business. She had changed the *belief system.*

It all began not with a strategy deck but with a simple question from a humble janitor:

"All well in the heart?"

In a world rushing toward deadlines, Bala had paused to ask something timeless. And in that pause, he had passed on the essence of leadership.

Vedika, once the regular manager, had become the corporate *catalyst.*

The final entry in her journal that evening read:

True leadership is not about being the smartest in the room, but about making the room feel seen, heard, and inspired.

And somewhere, as Bala swept the corridor humming his old folk tune, the building seemed to shine a little brighter. Not just from the polished floors, but from the uplifted hearts within.

Practices for the Corporate Spiritualist

1. **Mood Check Circles**: Before meetings, share a word that reflects your mood. Not to judge, but to witness.
2. **Energy Logs**: Reflect weekly on what lifted or drained you. Patterns speak louder than plans.
3. **Silent Acknowledgment**: Write a quick note in your diary, every time someone uplifts you, light it in your mind. Gratitude does not always need words.
4. **Listen with the Skin, Not Just Ears**: When someone speaks, listen not just to the words—but to the tremors or traces. That is where the truth lives.

The Corporate Raga

The workplace is not a machine. It is a raga—a melody woven by many notes. Emotional energy is its rhythm. To lead is not just to conduct tasks—it is to tune hearts. And when hearts are in harmony, strategy becomes symphony.

So the next time you walk into a meeting, do not just check the agenda. Check the energy. Listen for the unsaid. Look for the weary eyes, the hurried smiles, and the pause before a reply. In these silences, you will find your team's truth.

Because in every cubicle, every corridor, every call—there is a silent symphony playing. And it is yours to hear, shape, and respect.

The Calm Catalyst Truth #1:

"The emotional tone of a team meeting can shape its outcome more than any strategy document ever could."

CHAPTER 2

PATTERNS, NOT PEOPLE: THE POWER OF UNCONSCIOUS HABITS

2.1 Habits that shape team dynamics without being noticed

In the sleepy village of Narsipura, a place where the Hemavathi River sang melodies to the fields, life flowed not in hours and minutes but in seasons and stories. The fields were dumped with golden paddy, and at sunset, the scent of wet mud mingled with the distant sound of temple bells and the rhythm of wooden wheels on mud paths. Cows returned on their own from grazing, as if time had whispered their homecoming in their ears. But what ruled over this gentle chaos was neither the sun nor the stars—it was an old clock tower.

The clock tower was tall but weary, built by the British during the colonial days, long before Ravi Somanath's grandfather was born. Its paint had peeled off in layers, like the pages of time fading into memory. Its hands, stubborn and unpredictable, never pointed to the actual time. Some said the gears were rusted, others claimed a spirit lived inside, one that refused to align with the world's logic. Yet every hour, like an actor too proud to admit he forgot his lines, the clock tower rang its bells with solid confidence.

And somehow, the village believed it.

The 6 am chime, though actually closer to 5:15, prompted tea shops to open their shutters. The tea would bubble over a wood-fired stove, and men would gather with beedis between their fingers and silence in their eyes. At the 12 pm. toll, farmers turned their bulls back home, children rushed to the river, and women poured water from earthen pots onto stone steps, their bangles echoing like tiny temple bells. And every evening, the temple priest began the aarti at the bell's cue—even if the sun still waited above the hills.

No one questioned the clock. Over decades, it became the village's silent truth, like a myth everyone respected but no one dissected. Grandmothers told bedtime stories that began not with "Once upon a time" but "When the clock tower chimed at five..."

And for young Ravi, visiting Narsipura every summer from the city, it became a symbol. On one such visit, as he sat swinging under the jackfruit tree, his grandfather had whispered, "Watch the shadows, they'll show you what the sun hides." At the time, Ravi was too young to understand the meaning, but the sentence stayed with him like a perfume you can't name but always recognize.

Years turned, monsoons passed, and that boy grew up to be **Ravi Somanath**, a man with calm eyes and an analytical mind sharpened by business school and global exposure. He was recently appointed Director of Strategy at a leading technology firm in Bangalore—ArthaTech Solutions—a company known for its innovations but lately complained about for its internal fatigue.

On his first day, while others might have dressed in corporate flair, Ravi wore a quiet appearance. He rejected the traditional induction slideshow and polite welcomes. He did not want handshakes or cake in the conference room. Instead, he chose to roam the office—not as a leader claiming space, but as a traveller tracking path.

Ravi believed that culture did not sit in org charts. It breathed in what people did when no one watched. That is why, on Day One, he stood in a corner of the cafeteria with a paper cup, observing. He noticed who cleared their trays, who held the door, who checked their phones during conversations, and who nodded out of obligation.

The office was modern and buzzing, filled with glass partitions and creative posters—"Think Bold", "Fail Fast", "Lead with Empathy." But under the LED lights and ergonomic chairs, Ravi sensed something else—a tired rhythm. People moved fast, but not forward. Meetings were filled with jargon but lacked conviction. Dashboards blinked with activity, yet the air lacked energy.

The company seemed to be busy without momentum.

As he recalled his grandfather's phrase again—"watch the shadows"—Ravi realized those shadows were still there. But in the city, they did not fall from the sunlight. They fell from habits. Invisible, inherited, and unquestioned—just like the chimes of the clock tower.

Ravi began noticing patterns. Not grand ones, but micro-behaviours. In one department, everyone paused when a certain leader walked by. In another, juniors always walked behind their managers, even when there was no reason. During a weekly huddle, he observed how certain people spoke only after the "big voices" in the room had finished. And often, those who spoke first never asked questions—they only gave instructions.

One particularly revealing moment came on the third floor, near the finance bay. It was a Tuesday morning when Ravi happened to walk past a meeting room. He stopped, pretending to check something on his phone, but really, he was watching.

A young analyst named Jaya entered the room. She carried a file, a bottle of water, and a tense posture. She paused—not to greet anyone, but to glance at the seat closest to the door. Then she took it. Ravi's eyes followed the room as others trickled in. Her manager, Ramesh, came in with an aura of assumed authority and sat, as always, at the head of the table. Two other junior analysts sat near the back, diagonally across from Jaya. The centre of the table empty.

Not once did anyone claim the middle space. Even when there were only six people in the room, they spread like paint, avoiding the centre. Ravi had seen this too often. It was delicate, but it screamed hierarchy.

He returned to this room over the next two weeks. Not as a participant, but as a shadow, sitting quietly or peeking in through glass. And the pattern repeated like a ritual. The roles had been cast and costumes worn long before the curtain rose. Jaya always chose the same chair. Ramesh always opened the meeting. Juniors scribbled but seldom spoke. The centre remained a territory unclaimed.

And it was not just about furniture.

When Ramesh told a joke—dry, misplaced, and recycled—it drew polite laughter. Forced, thin, but present. Yet when Jaya once dared to share a humorous anecdote, it was met with silence. Not rejection. Not an insult. Just an awkward vacuum—as if laughter had a caste.

The room was not governed by policies. It was governed by invisible patterns.

Ravi returned to his desk that evening and opened his notebook, the one he carried not for notes, but for reflections. He scribbled a line that would later shape his entire leadership approach:

"This place is not broken. It is bound."

Bound by rituals, people no longer questioned. By habits formed from observation rather than intention. By unspoken rules of engagement that determined who had a voice, who had space, and who had silence.

In those moments, Ravi understood: This was the corporate version of the Narsipura clock tower. A system whose rhythm was respected despite its inaccuracy. Where everyone moved according to signals that no one verified. It was not a matter of fixing people—it was a matter of seeing the pattern.

And so, his mission began. Not with restructuring or vision decks, but with a quiet promise to himself: to notice the loops, the behaviours, the cultural habits that were shaping the company's momentum.

As the sun dipped below the horizon and the Bangalore skyline lit up like a circuit board, Ravi sat by the glass window, his fingers tracing the outline of a coffee cup. In that flickering reflection, he no longer saw just his own face.

He saw Narsipura.

He saw the clock tower.

He saw the invisible architects of time—not made of metal or wires, but of trust, fear, memory, and rhythm.

And he whispered, as if to the past,

"Sometimes, to fix a system, you do not need to change the clock.

You just need to remind people to ask—*is it even telling the right time?*"

2.2 Micro-interactions and Cultural Conditioning in Corporate Environments

After weeks of quietly mapping the invisible architecture of ArthaTech Solutions, Ravi began his next phase—not with department heads, but in the spaces often overlooked by leadership. He went to the pantry.

The air there was different. It carried the aroma of instant coffee, the soft clink of ceramic mugs, and the hum of casual, unfiltered conversations. Here, voices were not polished with jargon.

Ravi started with the admin staff, sharing a laugh about the ever-leaking coffee machine. He spoke with security guards, those silent guards who knew more about the office than most C-level executives. And in the stillness of early morning, long before sunrise, he met the night shift engineers—faces weary, eyes alert, voices heavy with stories never invited to daylight meetings.

What he found was not surprising—but it was sobering.

A pattern appeared—quiet but stubborn.

People responded to badges, not behaviours. The thin piece of plastic that dangled from a tag carried invisible power. Those with senior titles were treated differently—not rudely or with fear—but with a kind of social choreography that had become second nature. They were greeted more respectfully. People stepped aside in corridors. Even laughter around them came more measured.

This was not arrogance. It was not even intentional. It was conditioning—baked slowly into the workplace like the faint smell of disinfectant on polished floors. Over the years, these micro-interactions had encoded unspoken hierarchies far more powerful than any org chart.

And it went beyond greetings.

He noticed that most people did not finish their coffee. Not because they were busy—but because somewhere, someone had once said, *"Leisure shows lack of urgency."* That phrase had become ritual. So, sips were left mid-way, conversations were truncated, and cups sat half-drunk on spotless desks.

The desks themselves were neatly arranged, but not out of efficiency. It was a performance. Tidiness had become a visual indicator of discipline, not a tool of productivity. Everything in the workplace had a script, it seemed—right down to how one was supposed to appreciate someone.

Even recognition emails had a template. "Thanks for your outstanding contribution..." "Going above and beyond..."—phrases that had once meant something, now reduced to sterile copy-paste sentiments. What should have felt human had become mechanical.

Ravi returned to his desk and opened his brown journal, a quiet companion to his thoughts.

He knew he couldn't rewrite the entire structure. But he could change a single note. One ripple in the still water.

So, he decided to break a pattern. A small one.

Every Thursday, ArthaTech hosted a town hall in the central lobby—a glass-draped space that tried to look informal but far from the reality. Chairs were set in perfect symmetry. Senior leaders sat in the front row, mid-level managers behind them, and newer employees toward the back, heads bowed to their phones. Town halls had become ritualistic. Same format. Same applause. Same questions submitted in advance. Even the laughter came on cue.

But this Thursday, Ravi walked up to the mic—not with a performance, but with a question.

He adjusted the mic, looked around, and smiled gently.

"Who here remembers the last time they changed the route they took to work?"

There was a pause. A few awkward glances. Then, some hands went up—hesitant, like students unsure of the syllabus.

He continued:

"Why do we choose the same road—even when it is longer, jammed, or frustrating? Because it is familiar. Familiarity feels safe. But here is the thing—familiarity is the enemy of transformation."

Some smiled. Others frowned, unsure whether this was a philosophical monologue or a policy announcement.

"Next Thursday," Ravi said, pausing for breath, "I want each of you to swap desks for one day. Just a day. Sit next to someone you do not know. Someone in a different team. Talk. Not about work. But about habits. About your first job. About what makes you feel valued. Even what you hate about lunch options here."

You could feel the tension rise like a surge. Eyebrows lifted. HR leads exchanged glances. Someone near the back whispered, "This will mess up deliverables."

But Ravi stood his ground.

"We say we believe in collaboration, in cross-functional learning. But we rarely sit with unfamiliarity. If we want a culture that breathes, we must break its stuck ribs."

He walked away without asking for approval. That, he believed, would come from experience, not consent.

The next Thursday arrived like an exam day. People arrived early. HR volunteers had created a chart—random pairings. Backend developers sat next to brand designers. A quiet accounts analyst found herself beside a noisy sales executive. At first, the office looked like a misarranged jigsaw.

Awkwardness hung in the air—familiar, uncomfortable, yet promising. People sat uncomfortably. Introductions were mechanical. Some put on headphones, pretending to work. A few team leads hovered near managers, worried that the informal experiment would derail targets.

But by noon, something began to shift.

A backend engineer was seen explaining Python logic to a content writer, who asked out of curiosity, not as task. A UI designer and a payroll specialist laughed over shared stories of getting lost in Excel formulas. The accounts analyst and the sales executive exchanged stories about their childhood cities.

Someone played an old RD Burman song on a Bluetooth speaker.

Someone else offered homemade dishes.

Coffee was finally finished, not abandoned.

People were not speaking louder.

They were speaking differently.

The shift was not loud or dramatic. But it was real.

The day ended with smiles that were not curated. Some employees even suggested repeating the swap every month. Someone proposed "Crossover Coffee Thursdays." For the first time, collaboration was not a KPI—it was a conversation.

And Ravi? did not claim credit. He just returned to his journal and scribbled:

"Culture does not shift with banners and workshops.

It shifts when people are allowed to meet beyond roles.

To move from 'title' to 'touch point.'

From 'output' to 'outreach.'"

That night, Ravi walked through the nearly empty office. He paused at the desk of a young programmer who had left a sticky note: *"Fun day. Learned more in 3 hours than 3 months."*

In that moment, Ravi remembered his grandfather's words again.

"Watch the shadows. They will show you what the sun hides."

In the corporate corridors of power, the sun was always too bright—spotlighting targets, timelines, and performance dashboards. But shadows—they lived in patterns, in body language, in unfinished coffee cups. And sometimes, to create real change, you did not need a new strategy.

You just needed to ask the right question. And let the room answer.

2.3 Breaking Invisible Behavioural Loops

Ravi watched, saying little. He was not silent because he had nothing to say, but because the organization was already speaking—it always had been. Just not in words.

The changes over the past few weeks had been subtle. There were no reorg memos, no HR-led culture town halls, and no consultants offering three-point frameworks. Yet something had shifted. People sat differently. Talked differently. And, they *noticed*—not just screens and tasks, but each other.

And so, in his next internal email to the ArthaTech team, Ravi gave it a curious subject line:

Breaking the Clock Tower.

Some employees smiled when they read it. They remembered the town hall metaphor. Others were puzzled. But most opened the mail.

Inside, there was no corporate jargon. Just one paragraph:

"For years, a clock tower in my village rang its bell at the wrong time, but we followed it anyway. At ArthaTech, I see patterns that feel like that clock—familiar, confident, but not always right. Let us keep listening. Let us keep questioning. Let us keep noticing what we walk past."

No attachments. No KPIs. Just an invitation.

In the days that followed, Ravi replaced his leadership dashboard with a new metric—micro-interactions.

Not revenue-per-headcount.

Not agile stories closed per sprint.

Not pulse survey results.

But everyday signals of emotional and behavioural health.

He walked the floor with deliberate slowness, not to inspect, but to *observe*.

He noticed:

- How long did someone linger at the coffee machine? Was it a rushed gulp or a shared pause?
- Whether birthdays were remembered without Outlook reminders. Did people gather with presence or just show up because they had to?

- If the same people dominated airtime in meetings. And whether junior voices came with a hesitant tone or relaxed confidence.
- Whether laughter travelled beyond cubicles. Or was it muted, confined, like steam in a pressure cooker?

And in this clever noticing, something beautiful happened.

The loops began to weaken. Not because people tried harder. But because they noticed more.

A front-end developer who once kept to himself stayed longer at lunch.

A marketing lead began inviting a design intern to brainstorms.

And one day, for no apparent reason, someone brought a harmonica and played it at the evening break.

This was not the result of a "team bonding budget."It was the byproduct of people waking up inside a system that had numbed them.

One morning, as Ravi stood watching the rain from the glass corridor, an intern named Nisha approached him. She had wide eyes and a curiosity untouched by doubt.

"Sir," she said hesitantly, "what's your management philosophy?"

Ravi turned to her, smiled, and pointed to the floor tiles below their feet.

"Observe the tiles," he said. "Some are worn out more than others. That tells you where people walk the most. You do not need a survey to understand culture. You just need eyes."

Nisha hesitant slightly, tries to decode the metaphor. Ravi simply winked and walked away.

Later that day, she noticed something—how everyone used the same pantry door, though the other was closer for some. Habit. Pattern. Unquestioned loops. She wrote it down.

One evening, just as Ravi was about to leave, Ramesh—the finance head—walked into his cabin. His tie was loose, expression thoughtful, a change from his usual energy.

"You know," he began, settling into a chair uninvited, "something odd happened today."

Ravi looked up.

"Jaya led a meeting," Ramesh said. "I did not even realize I was not sitting at the head. It just… happened. She was already talking, and I just let it be."

There was silence.

Ravi did not rush to fill it. Finally, he said, "Not odd. Just new."

Ramesh giggled softly. "She was good. I mean, really good. Better than I have been in some of these updates."

Ravi just nodded. There was nothing to fix. The system was *self-healing* once the rigidity was softened.

As weeks turned into months, the change did not scream—it whispered.

ArthaTech did not just hit targets—they found something unique.

Momentum.

Not the frantic buzz of deadlines, but the internal pace of a place that had started to breathe again.

They had not added bean bags or new cafeteria snacks. There was no meditation app giveaway or Friday karaoke initiative. No motivational posters.

Instead, they rewired habits.

The marketing team, once known for solo presentations, now huddled daily with product leads—not because they had to, but because they wanted to avoid rework through better empathy.

Jaya began hosting monthly forums called "Break the Loop"—open spaces where employees could share any office ritual that felt outdated, pointless, or robotic.

One day, someone suggested removing the "Recognition Email Template" altogether and making handwritten notes instead.

Another day, someone turned the elevator waiting area into an art wall—where anyone could sketch or post a note about a colleague. It started with random doodles, but by the third week, it had become a canvas of gratitude.

In the quiet corner of the 4th floor, a wall was painted with a quote Ravi had once said offhand during a small group chat.

"We do not manage people. We manage patterns."

Around that time, a senior vendor visited the office for a pitch. He was sharp, well-prepared, and had done his homework. He walked Ravi through slides about talent attrition, engagement frameworks, and performance management.

At the end, he looked up and asked, "How do you keep people motivated without micromanaging?"

Ravi smiled and leaned back.

"The same way a farmer grows crops," he said.

"Not by shouting at seeds… but by preparing the soil."

The vendor was confused, unsure whether he had been complimented or challenged.

Not all changes were smooth. Not everyone embraced them.

Some senior leaders grumbled. "These soft things do not move revenue."

One department head sarcastically asked if the next deliverable review would be conducted via poetry.

And that's when Ravi realized something: People confused *activity* with *connection*.

The company celebrated birthdays with cakes and balloons, posted anniversary cards on MS Teams, Slack, and had a photo booth for "Employee Day." But these felt transactional—calendar events ticked off by a checklist-driven culture.

One day, a team forgot to bring a cake for a junior engineer's birthday. No one noticed. No one asked.

When Ravi found out, he did not call anyone.

Instead, he walked to the engineer's desk the next day and handed him a small handwritten note:

"Birthdays are more than events. They are reminders that people matter—every day, not just that day.

Thank you for being you."

That small gesture created waves. The engineer pinned it to his wall. Others saw it. Soon after, teams began celebrating not just birthdays, but life moments—a child's exam success, a teammate's first published poem, a designer's new rescue dog.

The calendar no longer dictated care.

Connection did.

It had taken just six months, but ArthaTech was a different place.

- Meetings began with people asking, "How are you—really?"
- A "Pattern Spotters Club" appeared gradually—employees who documented invisible norms and questioned them playfully.
- And Ravi? He kept walking slowly, smiling, an watching the dance of human systems, learning how to breathe again.

On the day he completed one year at ArthaTech, someone gifted Ravi a handcrafted miniature of a clock tower. The note attached read:

"It still doesn't tell the right time.

But it helped us find ours."

The Calm Catalyst Truth #2:

"Culture is not built by policies, but by patterns — the unseen rituals, reflexes, and repetitions that shape how people feel, think, and act when no one is watching."

CHAPTER 3

ENERGETICS IN THE ENTERPRISE: THE SCIENCE OF PRESENCE

3.1 Leadership Presence as an Energetic Phenomenon

In a land of steel and manufacturing, beyond the buzzing towers of Bengaluru and the smoke-tipped factories of Hosur, stood the headquarters of Geek2App Systems, a tech company often hailed as *"the engine behind the apps."* Its brand was unknown to the masses, but its code ran through the very traces of India's digital ecosystem. From ATM withdrawals to vaccine registrations, shipping trackers to health portals—if it blinked on a screen, Geek2App was behind it.

It was a company that made nothing the eye could see, yet everything the hand could feel.

Inside its ten-floor glass tower, thousands of minds toiled, tapping keyboards, attending daily stand-ups, chasing deadlines. Metrics were met. Reviews conducted. Bonuses issued. But something invisible, something vibrant, had gone missing.

Despite its grand digital muscle, Geek2App was in a state of quiet decline.

The numbers on the dashboards still looked decent. Profits were flat, not falling. Projects launched; clients renewed. But when CEO Harini Rao walked through the office, she saw it—the dimming of energy. People showed up but left early. Meetings were effective, but soulless. Conversations lacked colour, and celebrations felt orchestrated.

Projects ran, but not with passion.

Teams collaborated, but not in cohesion.

Promotions came, but leadership felt absent.

Harini could tell things were slipping. The data did not reflect it, but she knew—this was not a failure —but something worse. ***Stagnation***.

She was not the typical leader from B-Schools and bullet points. A trained engineer, Harini had once designed safety algorithms for drones. She stumbled into leadership when her team's project outshone others—and she was *nominated* for a leadership role, not by management, but by her own team.

She accepted it reluctantly, thinking, *"Maybe I can just make sure things don't break."* But over time, she realized what truly broke systems was not faulty logic. It was fatigue of the soul.

Her grandfather, a retired schoolteacher from Madurai, once told her on a humid summer evening:

"Even a silent room has a pulse, if you listen close enough."

At the time, it sounded poetic. Now, it felt predictive.

She began tuning herself to that idea.

The Rain That Changed the Season

It was on a rainy Monday morning—when clouds held to the city like dust and the building's glass panels reflected only grey—that Harini decided something had to shift.

During the all-hands town hall, she stood at the hall's circular podium, a space more used to celebrating milestones or showcasing demo days. She spoke without a slide.

"For the next 90 days," she declared, "we will measure not just productivity, but presence."

There was an awkward silence. A few exchanged glances. Presence? What did that even mean?

But Harini stood steady. Her voice was calm, like the one who had seen a truth others had not yet acknowledged.

"We will look for signals under the statistics. Feel the space between actions. This will not be about more work. It will be about more *being*."

Some rolled their eyes. Some grew curious. But everyone heard it—something was changing.

Her words rang like temple bells in a corporate jungle.

The Tale of the Three Directors

To begin, Harini turned her attention not to strategy decks or project pipelines, but to her three most senior leaders.

She called it her *listening tour*, though she did not tell them that.

She joined meetings as an observer. No titles. No agendas. Just the CEO quietly sitting, sometimes scribbling in her black notepad, sometimes just watching.

Vikram – Fire in a Suit

Vikram, the Head of Sales, was a force of nature. If meetings were weather, his were thunderstorms. He entered rooms with the gravity of a general and the urgency of an alarm. He spoke in numbers and deadlines.

"I want 20% growth. No excuses."

"They're delaying because we are not pressuring enough."

Under his leadership, sales soared. Yet so did resignations. Team members often asked for transfers. They respected him but feared him. He made them sharper—but smaller.

Harini watched him with a mix of respect and caution. *He burns so bright,* she thought, *but burns out everything around him, too.*

Sunaina – The Whispering Wind

Sunaina, Director of Operations, was the opposite. She moved through the office like a breeze—so quiet, she was often underestimated.

She listened more than she spoke. Her replies were gentle, often prefaced with "perhaps" or "let us explore." And yet, her department had never missed a major deadline in five years.

Her team worked like a flock of birds—no commands, just coordination. There were no theatrics, no loud appreciation posts. Just deep trust.

In one meeting, a junior executive forgot a crucial metric. Instead of being reprimanded, the team gently reminded him. No tension. No shame. Just recalibration.

Harini saw it and noted, *She does not command attention. She spreads belonging.*

Arvind – The Mirror of Water

Arvind, the Head of Product, was harder to interpret. He was like water—fluid, reactive, emotional.

In some meetings, he was extremely knowledgeable, full of metaphors and vision. In others, he seemed distracted, uncertain. His team adored him for his creativity but often felt adrift when clarity was needed.

His leadership reflected his environment. If the room was excited, he amplified it. If it was anxious, he absorbed it. But he rarely initiated a wave of his own.

Harini pondered. *He reflects beautifully. But does he shape anything?*

Decoding Frequencies

Over weeks, Harini sat through dozens of interactions. Not looking for content—but for *vibrations.*

She watched how people greeted each other in the corridors.

She noticed whose name was mentioned in meetings and whose absence was felt.

She sensed where laughter was spontaneous and where it was strategic.

A pattern began to form—not from reports, but from value.

Vikram created conflict. He pushed performance but also amplified stress.

Sunaina created importance. She valued effort and created space for quiet excellence.

Arvind created a reflection. He encouraged emotion but lacked a steady pulse.

And then it struck her—

Leadership was not a title; it was a frequency.

Each leader was like a tuning fork—vibrating at a frequency that either disturbed or aligned the collective field.

She recalled something she read in a forgotten book:

"Some frequencies interfere. Some amplify. Some heal."

Geek2App's problem was not a lack of talent or tech. It was *energetic noise.* Teams were playing notes—but not music. Everyone spoke, but no one resonated.

Presence, Not Performance

Harini began shaping a new language for leadership at Geek2App. One is not built around KPIs or OKRs, but around energy.

She coined the term **"Energetic Presence"**—a leader's ability to centre, ground, and elevates the collective mood simply by being.

She wrote in her journal:

"A present leader walks into a room and the room breathes better."

And so, instead of strategy offsite, she initiated "Silent Walks"—monthly sessions where senior leaders walked in pairs without talking for 20 minutes, then shared what they *noticed.*

Instead of performance reviews, she launched "Energy Maps"—a simple feedback tool where teams rated how aligned they felt on:

1. Cohesion – Do we feel synchronized or scattered?
2. Clarity – Do we know what matters, or are we guessing?
3. Care – Do we feel valued, or just used?

The Whisper Before the Wave

Not everyone understood it at first. Some called it "Leadership drama." Others mocked her "Zen CEO" approach.

But slowly, like a melody building from silence, something began to shift.

A senior engineer voluntarily mentored juniors.

A designer stayed late not out of pressure, but pride.

A usually silent intern started a Slack channel called Geek2App*Soul*—to share little acts of kindness happening across teams.

The Unseen Chisel

One evening, Harini sat alone in her office, looking at her grandfather's old chisel on her bookshelf. He had given it to her when she got promoted—saying:

"You may build apps, but never forget, the best leaders shape lives."

She now understood what he meant.

Leadership was less about steering the ship and more about tuning the wind.

The dashboard numbers would follow.

But first, the **frequencies** must align.

3.2 The Science of Presence

Every person in an enterprise is like a musical instrument. Each comes with a unique sound, a tone shaped by their experiences, mindset, and emotions. The organization, then, becomes a grand orchestra. Its rhythm is not set by the composer alone—but by the harmony among its players.

And just like in music, when one instrument plays even a fraction off-note, the entire melody trembles. It might still be technically correct, but it loses its soul.

That is what **Harini Rao** had come to understand—not through strategy slides, but by silently observing her people.

She realized that most organizations rewarded volume, visibility, and velocity. Yet what kept teams truly alive was *significance*. The quiet knowing that *we are in tune with each other*. That *what I do matters*, not just in outcome, but in intention.

The answer was not in KPIs—it was in *consistency*.

Presence Is Not Performance

In one of her leadership development circles, Harini shared a distinction that startled the room into silence.

"Presence is not charisma," she said, "it is consistency. It is the alignment of purpose, behaviour, and inner clarity."

A few raised eyebrows.

She went on:

"When a leader walks into a room, their energy speaks before their mouth does. The truly present do not seek attention. They centre the space."

This was not a motivational quote. It was a diagnosis. She had observed it countless times. In moments of chaos, some leaders calmed the room merely by showing up with quiet conviction. Others, even with inspiring speeches, left behind confusion and anxiety.

Presence was not about how loud you were. It was about *how aligned you were*—within yourself and with others.

The Start of the "Energy Map"

To make the invisible visible, Harini introduced a new practice across the entire Geek2App: the **Energy Map**.

It was deceptively simple.

Every team, at the end of the week, would answer just three questions—rated on a scale of 1 to 5:

1. **Consistency:** Did we feel in sync this week?
2. **Clarity:** Were roles, tasks, and priorities clear—not just written, but *felt*?
3. **Care:** Did we feel seen, heard, and supported?

No dashboards. No complex graphs. Just honest reflection.

Teams could submit anonymously. But over time, many chose to own their scores—and talk about them.

The Shock of Reflection

The first round of submissions came in. Harini and her core team pored over them late into the evening. What they saw was both shocking and enlightening.

One of the highest revenue-generating teams—hailed in internal forums as a "powerhouse"—scored 4.8 in Clarity, 4.5 in Consistency… and 1.7 in Care.

It was a jolt.

They were experienced, yes—but stiff. Conversations were transactional. Appreciation was rare. The team delivered, but the fear boiled under the surface. One anonymous comment read:

"We work like a machine. But machines do not need empathy."

On the other end of the spectrum, a team that had recently missed two client deadlines scored 4.9 in Consistency and 4.7 in Care, though their Clarity was low.

They were not failing. They were unfocused—but deeply connected. They joked in stand-ups. They helped each other without being asked. And when asked about the delays, they said, "We just need help aligning priorities. We are ready to fly."

It was not about performance metrics anymore. It was about *potential energy*—the kind that only flows when people feel safe and synchronized.

From Data to Dialogue

Rather than treat the Energy Maps as another reporting tool, Harini encouraged each team to use them as a **conversation starter**.

She set a rule: *Every team would spend 30 minutes every fortnight discussing their Energy Map as a group—no managers speaking first.*

The results were surprising.

In one team, a junior developer revealed she always stayed silent in meetings because she did not feel her ideas would be heard. She was stunned when three colleagues said they admired her perspective—and missed it.

In another, a veteran team lead broke down after hearing that his team saw him as "efficient but unapproachable." That week, he began having 10-minute weekly check-ins with every member—not to discuss work, but to ask: *"How are you, really?"*

People did not want perfection. They wanted *presence.*

The Healing Begins

Over the next 60 days, a subtle shift began rippling across Geek2App.

Meetings grew warmer, not longer. Laughter returned to the hallways. Slack channels stopped being just status updates and became places for support, gratitude, and even memes.

Harini watched it unfold like a monsoon after a long summer—first the scent of rain, then soft showers, and finally, a full downpour of human energy.

In one weekly leadership circle, a sceptical Delivery Head confessed:

"I used to think care was missing. But when my team scored it low, I sat down with them—and just listened. That one conversation improved delivery rate more than any Jira ticket ever could."

People were not burned out because of *too much work*. They were burned out because of *too little connection.*

Energy Whisperers and Emotional Architects

Harini noticed something else.

Some individuals—regardless of role or seniority—were natural Energy Whisperers. These were people whose mere presence in a room created ease. They calmed the tension with a joke. They asked the question no one dared to. They celebrated others without the need for attention.

She began recognizing and training them as Emotional Architects—the unseen framework of team culture. Not managers, not leaders-by-title—but *influencers of energy.*

They were coached on how to hold space in conflict, notice emotional signals, and reflect team mood in a healthy way.

These were the new custodians of culture. Not enforcers—but gardeners.

Rewriting What Matters

By the third month, something extraordinary happened.

A team in Hyderabad that had been flagged for restructuring was taken off the list—not because of a sudden spike in numbers, but because their Energy Map showed unprecedented growth in consistency and care.

Harini defended the decision:

"Let us not remove a limb just because it is slow. Let us treat the inflammation first."

That decision sent a powerful message: People were not disposable. Culture was not a luxury.

3.3 Aligning Purpose and Personal Frequency

Each carries a distinct character—shaped not just by skill or title, but by upbringing, beliefs, fears, and quiet ambitions. A sitar might have learned precision through pressure. A tabla may have found rhythm in resilience. A flute could be shy, yet piercingly clear in moments of purpose. These instruments arrive in meeting rooms, not in cases, but in cubicles.

And what do we expect of them?

We expect them to create harmony—not just alone, but together.

The organization, then, becomes a grand orchestra.

Its rhythm, opposite to what most corporate philosophies assume, is not set by the composer alone. Even the best CEOs, CHROs, or VPs cannot lead by policies alone. True orchestration depends on how the instruments listen to one another. How they pause. How they respond. How they *feel* their way through complexity.

And like in any orchestra, when even one player begins to play off-key—when their notes are distorted by anxiety, indifference, or unspoken conflict—the entire composition begins to tremble.

Not collapse. Just tremble.

It might still be technically correct. The project might close. The client might be happy. But something important—its *soul*—is missing. The symphony becomes a spreadsheet. The music, a metric.

That's what Harini Rao had come to understand—not through strategy slides or business reviews, but by simply watching people breathe.

She had spent two decades in technology, climbing the ladder, building platforms, making the invisible visible. But what no software tool or analytics suite had ever captured was *the energy between people*. The silent signals of mistrust. The vibrancy of care.

The weight of uncertainty on someone's shoulders on a Monday morning.

She came to a simple yet essential insight: What kept teams alive were not speed or scale—it was *resonance.*

Resonance meant more than rapport. It meant the quiet, often unconscious feeling that we are in tune with each other; that I am not alone, that what I say will be received, not just heard, that when I fall short, someone will notice—not to punish, but to understand.

In most companies, the rewards went to those who delivered *volume, visibility, and velocity*. The loudest voices. The flashiest presentations. The most emails were sent after 11 PM. But these were surface-level signals.

The real fuel was consistency—the alignment of people's purpose, behaviour, and inner clarity. Without it, even the best leaders generated noise instead of music.

3.4 The Idea of "Resonant" vs. "Dissonant" Teams

A **resonant team** is not one that avoids conflict—but one that *knows how to hold it.* Their disagreements do not affect the trust; they reveal truth. Just like the spaces between musical notes create meaning, it is the pause between differing opinions that creates understanding.

Conflict, when held with care, becomes creative friction—not the kind that tears apart, but the kind that shapes rough ideas into elegant ones. It was this texture that Harini Rao, the CEO of

Geek2App, longed to reintroduce into the cultural bloodstream of the organization.

Her insight came not from the usual organizational development playbooks, but from an old Carnatic concert she had once attended with her mother in Chennai. The vocalist and the violinist had exchanged improvisations for ten minutes—challenging, responding, and stretching the tune into new spaces. Not once did they break rhythm. Not once did the audience feel anxious. The interplay was alive, not aggressive.

That night, a single sentence had settled into Harini's heart like a raindrop on a copper bell:

"Harmony is not sameness. It is a shared commitment to listen."

This became the seed for what she would later call the **"Swarasya Circles."**

Birth of a Practice

The idea seemed at odds with the tech culture. Engineers and product managers were not known for spontaneous storytelling. Their calendars were filled with sprints, retros, and release calls. Time was currency—and no one was buying "emotional downtime."

But Harini persisted.

Every team in Geek2App was asked to dedicate 30 minutes every other week for a Swarasya Circle. The name, in Sanskrit, meant "of self-expression"—but also hinted at inner sound. The metaphor was intentional. This was not to be a status meeting or a knowledge share. No presentations. No "takeaways." Just stories.

Stories of work, yes—but also of life. Of what shaped people, what moved them, what mattered that week.

The initial reactions were mixed. Some managers joked about it being "mandatory mindfulness." Others called it "a corporate bonfire." Slack threads filled with memes. Engineers teased each other: *"Got a story for Swarasya, bro?"*

But as with all good music, the shift began not with noise, but with vibration.

When Walls Begin to Melt

In the third week of implementation, a Swarasya Circle in the Pune office became unexpectedly raw.

A quiet designer—who rarely spoke in meetings—shared a memory. Her father had passed away a few months ago. She had not taken extended leave. She had not told many. But one afternoon, she received a short message from someone in HR: *"Take all the time you need. We are holding the fort."*

She read it aloud, her voice trembling. "It was not long. But that mail told me I was not invisible."

The room was still. One backend developer looked away, swallowing something behind his glasses.

After the circle, he messaged her: *"My father died during lockdown. I never told anyone. Thank you for giving me permission to grieve."*

In another team, a tech lead spoke—without the dramatics—about feeling invisible as a leader. He said he had begun to wonder if his work even mattered, beyond Jira tickets. Several teammates interrupted—something rare for them—to thank him for the late-night bug fixes, the calm presence on client escalations, and the snacks he always stocked in the pantry.

He smiled. He did not say much after that. But the next day, he changed his Slack status for the first time in a year. It simply read:

"Not just fixing bugs. Building trust."

From Ritual to Rhythm

By the end of two months, Swarasya Circles evolved from obligation to retreat.

Some teams added music to their sessions—one began with a 2-minute playlist; another ended with someone reading a poem or quote. Some preferred silence before speaking. Others adopted a talking object—a shared pen, a small clay bird, a Rubik's cube—that one held when they spoke, and passed on gently.

Harini was careful not to formalize any of this. The power of Swarasya lay in its unforced, fluid nature. Like breath, it had to move in and out without rigidity.

Over time, managers stopped resisting. They noticed something unusual:

- Tense stand-ups became easier.
- People began owning their misses without fear.
- Juniors started voicing product ideas earlier in the sprint, instead of waiting for design to freeze.

The change was not seismic. It was faint, but deep—like the way air feels lighter after rain.

In one quarter-end review, a veteran delivery manager said,

"We did not reduce errors by fixing the process. We reduced them because people stopped pretending."

When Business Becomes Personal (In the Best Way)

As Swarasya matured, stories deepened.

A newly joined graduate trainee shared that he did not feel "good enough" to be on the team. He admitted he had considered quitting. He was shocked when a senior architect told him, *"You remind me of my younger self. You ask questions I have forgotten to ask."*

A QA lead shared her fear of turning 40 and becoming "irrelevant" in a 20-something tech world. The team not only reassured her—they created a mentorship pairing program the next month, where juniors could learn real-world system insight from seniors who had *seen* the backend of scale.

These were not "employee engagement" initiatives.

They were emotionally shaping.

When people felt heard without being fixed…

When stories were received without judgment…

When vulnerability stopped being rare and became cultural currency…

Teams transformed from effective machines to human mosaics.

The Turnaround

Nine months into this energetic renaissance, Geek2App began to change.

Attrition dropped. Innovation spiked. But more than that, hallways echoed with laughter. People lingered after meetings. Leaders listened with their bodies, not just their ears.

Harini received a letter from a junior developer, Shravan.

"I came to Geek2Appfor a job. I found a frequency I did not know I had. Thank you for tuning us."

She smiled and looked at her grandfather's old chisel on her desk. The legacy of shaping—not products, but presence.

The Calm Catalyst Truth #3:

"Leadership is not a role but a resonance. When purpose aligns with presence, energy flows. And when energy flows, enterprises flourish."

PART II

MICRO-MECHANICS OF MEANING

CHAPTER 4

RITUALS OF THE UNSPOKEN: FROM MONDAY MOODS TO MEETING MANNERS

4.1 The role of micro-rituals in creating psychological safety and trust

A high-rise building in Gurugram, on the twenty-second floor, there was an IT product company named Nivara. It was not known for flashy branding or unicorn status. Yet, its employee retention rate was among the best in the industry. No formal research had captured this, and no HR paper had recorded it. It was simply known by those who worked there.

The secret was not in their ESOPs or gym memberships. It was not their flexible hours or hybrid model. It was something else, "rituals that nourish the spirit more than the system."

The Monday Gaze

Every Monday, before the sprint planning meeting, the team at StudioQ—a small but high-impact design unit inside Nivara

—gathered not to discuss Jira boards or release cycles, but to participate in a peculiar ritual known only to them as the "Monday Gaze."

It was not on any official calendar. There was no formal invite. It did not block anyone's time on Outlook. And yet, without fail, at 9:08 AM, people trickled into the soft-cushioned lounge outside the war room. Nobody questioned the odd timing—9:08, not 9:00. Someone had once joked that "great ideas arrive eight minutes late." That stuck.

At the centre of the lounge sat a low wooden table, worn and carved with initials from years past. On it, a small brass diya was lit—not for prayer, but for presence. It flickered quietly, its flame never seeking attention, much like the ritual itself. This was not about religion or HR initiatives. It was about rhythm. Slowing down to tune in.

Parth, the team's manager, never called himself a leader. "I'm a listener who sometimes types," he would say. But on Mondays, he held space with quiet authority. He asked just one question—always open-ended, always deceptively simple:

"How's the weather in your mind today?"

That was it.

No "how are you doing" or "what's the update." Just a gentle nudge toward self-awareness. And people answered—not with performance metrics or weekend summaries—but with metaphors that peeled back the surface.

"Cloudy with a chance of conflict. My son's school drama spilled into my headspace."

"Sunny, but a bit dry. Need some inspiration."

"Foggy. I know I'm here, but not fully."

"Thunderstorms last night. Still clearing."

Sometimes there was laughter. Sometimes, a pause heavy enough to quiet even the vending machine hum. Parth never responded with solutions. No coaching, no fixing. He just nodded, lit the second diya on the side table, and let silence do the real work. That silence was the invisible container in which people felt seen, without being exposed.

There were no notes taken. No action items. Yet, what unfolded in that half-hour bled into the rest of the week. Conflicts were defused before they formed. Slack threads grew kinder. A junior once mustered the courage to disagree in a product call—and was met with genuine curiosity instead of defensiveness.

This ritual had a ripple effect. Tuesday stand-ups got sharper. Wednesday check-ins are more honest. And Friday wrap-ups, often celebratory, began to acknowledge not just wins, but wounds—mistakes owned without fear.

The Monday Gaze was the first of many such micro-rituals. Some were quiet, like this one. Others are more playful—like "Mistake Mornings" on Thursdays, where someone wore a hat shaped like a red question mark and shared their biggest goof-up of the week. No judgment. Just laughter. And learning.

These rituals were never documented in a handbook. They did not show up in leadership dashboards. But they held the culture together like the invisible threads in an heirloom sari—not loud, but untearable.

Because, in the end, trust is not built in workshops or strategy decks.

It is woven, one honest metaphor at a time

The Chair That Changed Everything

In the glass-walled conference room named *Kurukshetra*—a name that felt too dramatic for quarterly reviews but strangely appropriate—there was a single red chair placed oddly in the corner. It did not match the rest. While the others were sleek, ergonomic, and aligned tightly around the table, this one faced slightly away, angled toward the window. Almost like it was listening to a conversation happening outside the room.

This chair had no label. No plaque. No HR memo explaining its purpose. But everyone in the company knew what it meant.

It was called *the Question Chair.*

The origin was simple and almost accidental. Months ago, during a heated debate about marketing spend, Meera, a junior analyst with less than a year at the firm, had stood up mid-meeting and walked to that corner. From there, she had softly asked, "What if we were solving for the wrong problem?" The room had gone silent. The tension, which until then felt like two armies locked in battle, suddenly turned inward. Her question did not derail the meeting—it re-centred it.

Since then, the chair remained.

Every strategic review that followed began with a new ritual. One team member—chosen at random, sometimes volunteered—would sit in the red chair. Their role was not to present, not to argue, and definitely not to convince. Their only task?

To ask questions.

That is it.

No answers. No counterpoints. Just thoughtful, open-ended inquiries meant to stir reflection.

Why are we prioritizing this feature and not that one?

If our competitor made the same move, how would we react?

Who is not in this room, and how might they see this plan?

What part of this strategy feels more like fear than purpose?

Sometimes the questions were simple. Sometimes they were unsettling. Sometimes, they poked at egos that weren't ready to be questioned. But over time, something began to shift. The red chair changed the very texture of the meetings.

Executives—who once came armed with slides, numbers, and slogans—began arriving with stories, with doubts, and, increasingly, with humility. They were not just bracing for applause or alignment. They were preparing for an inquiry. And not just from investors or customers—but from their own people.

The Question Chair had created something rare: a space where curiosity was more powerful than certainty.

It also exposed an invisible truth about most corporate settings—meetings are often dominated by those with the most confidence, not the most clarity. The red chair flipped this norm. Here, the quietest voice had the loudest role.

One time, a new intern asked, "If this project succeeds, who benefits the least?" The question haunted the room. Not because it was rebellious, but because no one had thought of it.

People began to listen differently. Not just to words, but to what was missing between them.

In time, the red chair became a symbol—not of hierarchy, but of humility. It reminded everyone that true leadership is not about having the answers.

Sometimes, it is about making space for the right questions.

And in a room called *Kurukshetra*, what better weapon than wisdom dressed as wonder?

The Art of the Shared Pause

Every Friday at exactly 3:33 PM, something curious happened in the bustling open office of Arya Systems. In the middle of keystrokes, meetings, dashboards, and deadlines, a small brass bell rang—not from a speaker, not part of a system notification, but rung by hand.

The bell was rung by the youngest intern on the floor.

It was not ceremonial. It was not announced. It was not even on the official calendar. Yet when that bell rang—just one soft chime that cut through the buzz of a thousand tasks—everyone paused. Literally. Everyone.

This was *The Pause.*

For 3 minutes and 33 seconds, there was no talking, no typing, no Teams pings, no multitasking. People simply… stopped.

There were no instructions, no posters, and no mindfulness manuals. And that was the beauty of it. Each person experienced *The Pause* in their own way. Some closed their eyes and let their shoulders drop. Others stood by the window and let their gaze drift across the skyline. A few scribbled thoughts into small notebooks—poems, worries, or single words that made no sense but felt important. Some simply sat with their coffee and listened to their own breath for the first time all week.

It was a collective exhale in a culture obsessed with inhale.

It had started quietly six months ago. Parth, the unit's leader, had returned from a retreat—not a flashy leadership one, but a quiet weekend he spent alone in his childhood village. He came back with no presentations, no frameworks. Just a bell in his hand and an idea in his heart.

The first Friday, when he rang it, people laughed. Some were confused. But he said nothing. He only asked for 3 minutes and 33 seconds. That number was not random—it was just odd enough to feel intentional and playful, not rigid.

Soon, the ritual caught on. Slowly. Gradually. People began to look forward to it. It was not seen as a productivity hack. It was not branded as mindfulness. It was simply… permission.

Permission to pause.

One Friday, a guest from a partner company was visiting and happened to witness *The Pause*. As the bell rang and conversations melted into silence, she looked around—confused, intrigued. After the silence lifted and people resumed their work, she walked up to Parth and asked, "What exactly does this bell achieve?"

Parth smiled and said softly, "It reminds us we are not machines. Machines are designed to run endlessly. But humans? Humans pause. That is not a flaw. That is our wisdom."

The visitor did not reply. But later that week, she ordered a bell online.

And back at Arya Systems, people noticed something curious: that the few minutes of stillness every Friday somehow made the noise of the week feel more meaningful. Like the silence between musical notes. Without *The Pause*, perhaps the music would just be noise.

Over time, The Pause became more than just a break. It became a mirror—reflecting not how much they were doing, but *how* they were being.

And sometimes, in that 3 minutes and 33 seconds, someone found an answer they did not know they were seeking.

Invisible Contracts: A Story of Mahima and the Mug

Mahima was a senior engineer—meticulous, dependable, and often mistaken for just another part in the company's well-oiled delivery machine. She was not the loudest in the stand-ups, nor the first to take credit in retros. She was the kind of presence people felt only in her absence—quiet power, the type that held teams together from the inside.

Her one-year work anniversary came and went like any other sprint day. No automated email from HR. No confetti on the Slack channel. Just a regular Thursday, with deadlines to meet and code to push.

She had not expected much, really. But as she returned from a short tea break, there it was on her desk—a small potted *tulsi* plant, wrapped simply in brown paper with a string bow.

Attached was a folded note in neat handwriting:

"In this team, you're not just code—you're culture."

Mahima paused, a little confused. Then she noticed the ceramic mug beside it. A plain white cup, but not store-bought. It was handmade—uneven in shape, painted roughly with bold strokes of colour, and on it, a mess of scribbled signatures and notes in permanent marker.

From every member of her team.

"Mahima, your calm saved my chaos on Deployment Day."

"Your code is poetry."

"Thanks for always being the anchor during madness."

Even the office helper had written, "Always smiled. Even on tough days. That matters."

It was not official merchandise. It did not have the company logo. But it carried something far deeper—memory, attention, affection.

Mahima smiled, a rare, wide smile that warmed her entire face. She looked around. Kabir stood nearby, pretending to scroll through his phone. It was clear who had done this. But no big speech followed. No announcement. Just a quiet nod.

Later that evening, Mahima asked Kabir, "Why did you do this?"

He shrugged. "It is just something we do."

No one had trained Kabir. No checklist had asked him to remember someone else's work anniversary. But he remembered—because someone had once remembered his. On his own one-year mark, two years ago, he, too, had received a plant and a mug with scribbled notes.

Back then, it was Meenu who had done it for him. And she, in turn, had once been surprised by Nand. No emails. No workflows. Just a thread of thoughtful action carried forward. Quiet. Consistent. Human.

It had become a ritual—not a rule. A soft tradition passed not through policy but through behaviour. An invisible contract, inked not with compliance, but care.

And over seven years, this silent lineage had grown. No documentation existed. Yet it was more powerful than any KPI. More binding than any process.

In the end, Mahima did not care that the HR automation had missed her. What stayed with her was the sense that she mattered. Not just her productivity, but her presence.

And that is what rituals do at work—they whisper what policies forget to say:

You are not just here to work. You are here to belong.

From Rituals to Resonance

In the corner of the company cafeteria, placed between the humming vending machine and the espresso counter, hung an old whiteboard—worn out at the edges and framed with tape to keep it from wobbling. It was not company-issued. It was not on any process chart. No one really remembered who put it up. Some said it was a former product manager who had once read something about "vulnerable spaces." Others claimed it just appeared one day, like a spontaneous act of architecture. But one thing was certain—it stayed.

Above the board, in child-like permanent marker, someone had scrawled a header:

"Write What You Can't Say."

There were no rules. No approvals. No logins. Just one whiteboard marker tied to a string and an unspoken understanding. People wrote sentences. One line at a time. No names. No context.

By Monday morning, it was always wiped clean.

But by Friday afternoon, it was full of heartbeats.

Some were cryptic, like a corporate riddle:

"I wish someone asked how I really am."

"We moved the milestone, but not the burnout."

Some were gently humorous:

"Still waiting for Jira to track my emotions."

"My code compiles, but I do not."

Some were painfully raw:

"I am scared I am losing the fire."

"Silence in meetings does not mean agreement. It sometimes means exhaustion."

And some were quietly celebratory:

"Today I found joy in debugging."

"My intern taught me something magical."

Nobody knew who wrote what. That was the magic. The anonymity removed ego and spotlight. What remained was honesty—unfiltered, undressed, and deeply human.

One week, someone wrote:

"I cried in the washroom. Twice."

No explanation. No plea. Just a simple declaration.

The next day, someone else responded back with a new line:

"You are not alone. I cried in the server room once. It is quieter there."

Soon, the board was not just a surface. It was a collective soul.

Engineers, marketers, HR folks, facilities staff—everyone stopped by, even if just for a minute. They did not always write, but they read. And when they read, they paused. And when they paused, something shifted.

In a world obsessed with speed, this board slowed people down.

Parth, the team manager known for his emotional intelligence, once described it as "our shared whisper." He would bring visiting clients by and show them—not the OKR dashboards, but this board. "This," he would say, "is our culture in ink."

It was not about venting. It was about visibility. Emotional visibility.

In one particularly intense week—when layoffs had shaken the building and trust hung low—a single sentence appeared on the board:

"I survived. But it feels like survivor's guilt."

No one erased it. Not even on Monday. That line stayed an extra week. It was sacred.

One morning, a new employee named Tarini stood in front of the board, coffee in hand. She had not yet made friends. She did not fully understand the company's rituals. But when she read a line that said,

"Learning to find my worth outside my output,"

her eyes welled up. She did not write anything. But she returned the next day. And the day after. And then, on her 30th day, she added her own:

"It took me 29 days to believe I belong."

The board was not just an emotional release—it was silent on boarding. Culture transmission without a handbook. Leadership without hierarchy.

People began making time in their calendars: "5 min – Whiteboard Walk." What was once a quirky corner turned into a sacred pause. Some teams even discussed the board during retrospectives—not to solve, but to acknowledge.

Once, a sceptical senior executive—rigid, suit-clad, number-driven—walked past the board with a junior colleague. He giggled and said, "Is this where people dump their drama?"

The junior employee replied gently, "No, sir, it is where we pick up our empathy."

The executive stood silently, reading the lines. Something softened in his face. That Friday, someone wrote:

"My father passed last year. This week was his birthday. did not tell anyone at work. But I carried it all day."

Right below it, in slightly shaky writing, was a reply:

"Same here. Thank you for saying it out loud."

This was not a feedback loop. There were no KPIs, no color-coded action items. It was not a tool. It was a *tone.*

These were emotional murmurs in a noisy enterprise. And yet, they reverberated far louder than quarterly memos or vision statements.

Because while buildings need architects, cultures need listeners.

And in this company, above the coffee machine, amid the clatter of mugs and the rush of deadlines, a simple whiteboard had become a mirror—one that reminded everyone: behind every badge is a beating heart.

4.2 Ceremonies, daily practices, and invisible contracts at work

The Pause That Connects

At **Nivara Systems**, there were no big moments for medals, no emails that started with "It gives me great pleasure," and certainly no cake-cutting ceremonies with HR leaning in for photographs. Yet, once in a while, something would shift quietly in the air—like the hush before the first monsoon rain.

It wasn't a birthday or a product launch. It was something smaller. Quieter.

It was recognition.

Not the kind you frame and hang. But the kind that makes you sit up straighter—without realizing it.

Take the story of **Leena**, a technical writer who joined three years ago. Quiet, precise, and always a little behind the scenes. She documented the most complex workflows in a language so simple, the most chaotic developer could understand it.

But Leena wasn't the type who raised her hand in meetings. Or chased deadlines with noise. She moved like water—without resistance, without drama.

One Thursday morning, after a week of intense system outages and recovery documentation, she noticed something different. Her manager, **Rohit**, paused at her desk—not for a stand-up update or a pending ticket. He just stood there with a cup of tea, eyes soft.

He didn't say much.

Just this:**"I've been watching. You've grown. Not just in your work—but in how you hold the team when things fall apart."**

That was it.

No designation change. No salary letter. No calendar invite marked "Manager Connect." Just those words. Measured. Slow. And oddly unforgettable.

Later that evening, Leena didn't post about it on LinkedIn. She didn't tell her parents. But she quietly reordered her desk. Removed two old Post-it notes filled with self-doubt. Replaced them with one:

"Steady is also strong."

The next morning, she came in early, left a handwritten note on the team whiteboard:

"Here's to the quiet ones who hold the fort while the world shouts."

Beside it, a box of snacks from her hometown in Tamil Nadu.

No name. No hint.

But everyone knew.

Because in teams that breathe with care, recognition doesn't need fireworks. It just needs sincerity.

Across the floor, **Dev**, a product designer battling burnout, noticed it. He smiled. For the first time in weeks, he stayed back an extra 30 minutes to help QA on a ticket. Not because anyone asked—but because *something in the silence had reminded him why he cared.*

In the weekly review, Rohit mentioned Leena's name. Not with praise, but with gratitude.

"Sometimes, the strongest systems aren't built in sprints. They're built in the spaces between crises—held by people who never ask for credit."

That evening, during the chai break, Leena shared a small story from her college:

Her professor once told her, *"You may not lead the parade. But you will carry the map."*

She never forgot that. She didn't chase the spotlight. She just kept mapping.

And that, in many ways, was the heartbeat of Nivara.

Recognition here wasn't designed for scale. It was designed for sincerity.

There was Ramesh, the office admin, who kept refilling the pantry with everyone's unspoken preferences. When asked why he did it, he just said, "People work better when they're quietly cared for." One day, someone left a thermos of filter coffee on his desk with a note: *"You notice us. We notice you, too."*

Or Sara, a senior analyst, who once sat with a new intern for four hours to help him find confidence in his first data story. No manager saw it. But word travelled—through gratitude, not gossip.

At Nivara, growth was not a title. It was a turn in posture. A shift in rhythm. A subtle widening of someone's view.

When someone grew, it didn't echo in inboxes. It showed up in how others leaned into them. How they became *someone people trusted, not because of a rank, but because of how they listened.*

There was no "Thank God It's Friday" themes. But there were many Mondays that began with more energy because someone, somewhere, had felt *seen.*

Managers here didn't wait for appraisals to acknowledge transformation. They shared it—on break walks, over shared umbrellas, next to Coffee machines filled with the aroma of chaos.

And when they did, they often left behind more than words.

They left behind belief.

As one old-timer once said during a team offsite:

"You don't need to be loud to be seen. You just need someone willing to notice beyond your output."

In the tradition of Nivara, the loudest kind of praise was this kind of pause.

It didn't shout your growth.

It mirrored it back to you.

Because the most honest kind of coaching isn't always a workshop or a template.

It's a person pausing just long enough to let you know:

"You've become more than your role. And I see you."

Why These Rituals Matter

The Little Things That Make Big Things Work

Let's be honest. Most of us do not wake up thinking, "Oh wow, today I'm going to be part of a micro-ritual." No. We wake up thinking about traffic, unread emails, and whether the coffee machine will finally work without spitting out something weird.

But here's the thing. Micro-rituals—those tiny, often overlooked practices—might just be the difference between a place you work at and a place you belong to.

Let me tell you about **Team Nexus**—a product team at a tech company in Bangalore, somewhere between the startup energy and corporate structure. It was not Google, but it was not a no-name either. They had deadlines, pressure, Jira tickets, and the occasional "fix ASAP" from leadership.

But they also had *something else.*

Every Wednesday morning, before the team stand-up, they would have a "Check-In Circle." Just 10 minutes. One person would light a little scented candle (lemon grass, usually), and each team member would share one non-work thing that was on their mind.

Sometimes it was deep. "My mom's biopsy report is due today."

Sometimes silly. "I forgot to put on deodorant."

Sometimes random. "I watched *3 Idiots* again and cried like a baby."

There was no judgment. No fixing. Just listening.

And you know what? Those 10 minutes did more for team bonding than three months of "collaboration training."

These were **micro-rituals**. Not officially sanctioned by HR. Not added to any productivity metric. But they were the *soul glue.* They stitched a feeling of "we are in this together" without anyone having to say it out loud.

You might wonder—why does any of this matter? Why not just get the work done and go home?

Because humans are not routers. We do not just pass data. We carry emotions. And in a high-stress environment like the modern workplace, emotions—if not acknowledged—become noise. Micro-rituals are like noise-cancelling headphones. They bring in rhythm. And rhythm brings trust.

Think about it.

When you see a colleague place their hand on your shoulder just before your big presentation, unspoken ritual. When your team leaves one chair empty during retros to remind themselves of the customer, unspoken ritual. When someone always brings two extra pens to meetings, "just in case someone forgets"—ritual again.

Rituals create rhythm.

Rhythm creates trust.

Trust creates safety.

And safety creates performance.

Simple chain. But ignored by many.

Companies spend crores on consultants to "build culture." Culture decks. Vision workshops. Leadership retreats in Goa. But the truth is, culture is not a workshop. It is what happens after the workshop.

Like when Priya from Design always shares one meme in the Monday morning thread. Or how the team has a bell that rings every time someone makes a mistake—but only so that they can say, "Thank you for owning it."

Nobody teaches these things. They're not in the on boarding slideshow. But they spread—like oral tradition. From senior to junior. From observer to doer. They're caught, not taught.

And here's the coolest part—they're not always designed. Sometimes, they just occur.

At Nivara, there was this guy, Ramesh. He did not talk much. But every time a new intern joined, he would give them a "Beginner's Pack"—three post-it notes with handwritten tips:

1. Ask "why" even when people look annoyed.
2. Never eat lunch alone.
3. Save your code, save your sanity.

It was not an HR mandate. No manager told him to do it. But over two years, *that* became a ritual. Now every senior engineer had their own version of the Beginner's Pack. No meetings were needed. It became... rhythm.

And here is what most leaders do not realize: **micro-rituals are power-neutral**. You do not need a VP title or a budget. Anyone can start one. That intern who rings the brass bell at 3:33 PM every Friday to remind people to pause? He's more influential than half the middle managers walking around with Gantt charts and grumpy faces.

Because when people feel *seen*, they do not just work. They care. And caring leads to magic.

Now, let me be real, rituals alone won't save a toxic company. If your boss screams at you and then gives you a cupcake, it is not a ritual—it is manipulation. Rituals work when they come from a place of authenticity, not control.

So next time you see someone do something meaningful—even if it seems small—do not brush it off as fluff. That smile at the end of the call, that "how are you really?", that silly Friday pun thread... these things *matter.*

Because in the end, we do not remember every slide we saw or every tool we used. We remember the way a place made us *feel.*

And micro-rituals? They're the secret recipe for that feeling.

So maybe, just maybe, the next time you walk into work, do not ask, "What do I need to do today?"

Ask, "What rhythm am I part of?"

And better still—"What ritual can I start?"

It does not have to be grand. It just has to be real.

And that, my friend, could be the beginning of a culture shift.

The Calm Catalyst Truth #4:

"The strength of a culture is not in its rules, but in its rituals."

CHAPTER 5

THE HYGIENE OF THE MIND – COGNITIVE CLUTTER AND EMOTIONAL TOXICITY

5.1 Emotional hygiene as a corporate necessity

The human mind is the most overutilized yet under-maintained tool in our professional arsenal. We often prioritize clean desks, organized files, and structured calendars—but what about the internal workspace? The mental desktop? In a society that celebrates productivity and cognitive sharpness, we have forgotten a crucial discipline: emotional and mental hygiene.

Part I: The Inner Workplace

A high-rise building in Bengaluru, the headquarters of a booming fintech startup, buzzed with the energy of deadlines. Every morning, Aman, a 34-year-old team lead, walked in, nodded to his colleagues, sipped his cutting chai, and sat at his meticulously organized desk. Outlook launched. Slack lit up. Stand-up meetings. Follow-ups. Calls. More calls. From the outside, he looked like the poster boy of productivity.

But inside his head? Chaos.

Thoughts from yesterday's tense client call still played on loop. A tinge of guilt from the rushed conversation with his son that morning. Frustration from an unacknowledged idea shared two weeks ago. Anxiety about tomorrow's presentation. Like most professionals, Aman wore an invisible mental backpack—heavy, cluttered, and unaddressed.

Walk into any office in Mumbai, Gurgaon, or Bengaluru, and you'll see a similar script: structured rituals masking unstructured minds. Behind neat workstations and polite small talk lie racing thoughts, subtle emotional wounds, cognitive shortcuts, and mental fatigue. The office may look organized. The mind often is not.

Here's the truth we don't speak enough of in Indian boardrooms: our minds are running outdated software riddled with bugs—biases, overthinking, self-doubt, and suppressed emotions. And like a smart phone with too many apps open, we eventually lag. We crash. Not visibly. But silently.

We are never taught how to maintain our inner world. No school trains us to process emotional residue. No MBA curriculum teaches how to declutter mental chaos. But the consequences are real. Emotional toxicity—resentment, imposter syndrome, fear of failure—seeps into how teams collaborate, how managers decide, how innovations die in silence.

Nobel laureate Daniel Kahneman spoke of two systems in our brain. System 1—fast, automatic, impulsive. System 2—slow, deliberate, reflective. Most of corporate life runs on System 1. It is efficient, but it is also lazy.

Here's where the Indian cultural context becomes important. We are raised to maintain harmony. Do not question. Do not complain. Keep calm. Respect hierarchy. While this promotes teamwork, it also chokes expression. People swallow frustrations. They suppress doubts. What is not expressed irritates. And suppressed emotions quietly fog judgment.

Radha, a young analyst, disagrees with her manager in a team meeting. But she stays silent, out of respect—or fear. That disagreement stays inside her, unresolved. Over time, it breeds disconnection. She stops sharing ideas. The team loses out—not just on productivity, but perspective.

Mental clutter is not always dramatic. It is subtle. A delay in responding to emails. A hesitation to take initiative. An overreaction to feedback. These are symptoms. The cause? Poor mental hygiene.

In Indian homes, we clean thoroughly before festivals. Cobwebs are removed. Corners scrubbed. The home shines. What if we did the same for our minds? What if organizations had rituals to sweep away emotional residue, clean mental cobwebs, and refresh the cognitive atmosphere?

Here's the starting point: acknowledge that mental hygiene is not a luxury. It is a necessity. Just like we update antivirus software on our devices, we need regular check-ins, reflective pauses, and emotional processing in our workdays.

Companies do not fall apart from bad strategies. They fall apart from poor emotional environments—unspoken tensions, unresolved conflicts, and unmanaged stress. Clarity, not just intelligence, drives performance. And clarity comes from the cleanliness of thought.

In the chapters ahead, we'll explore techniques from cognitive science and Indian spiritual traditions that show us how to clean the mind. But before that, let's plant a seed:

What if the real productivity hack is not working harder, but thinking clearer?

So, the next time you sip your morning chai and open your inbox, pause. Ask yourself—not "What must I finish today?" but "What must I clear today?"

Because a clean mind does not just work better. It sees better. And sometimes, that is all we need to lead—not with pressure, but with peace.

Part II: Emotional Hygiene as a Corporate Necessity

Let me take you to a building in Bengaluru—not the tall glass kind you see in calendars, but the one behind a dusty metro pillar, where dreams are coded in silence.

Inside, on the 8th floor, Aman sits at his desk.

He's thirty-four, punctual, polite, and perpetually on time. His inbox is clean. His shirt is always crisp. Every task is neatly logged in Trello. To the world, Aman is a machine of discipline.

But here's the twist.

Inside his mind? Total chaos.

There are no alarms for mental overload. No sticky notes reminding you to "Clear emotional residue." Yesterday's client argument replays on loop. The guilt of leaving his son mid-sentence this morning pokes him like a forgotten notification. A great idea he shared last week still lies unread—buried under the hierarchy.

The truth? Aman is not alone.

Walk into any Indian office—in Gurugram or Guindy, Powai or Pune—and you'll find order on the outside, but unseen mess within. Just like our laptops run silently hot, most minds hum with unspoken noise: unsaid apologies, quiet frustrations, old wounds dressed in new formals.

In India, we clean homes before Diwali. We wash doors, beat the carpets, and even dust behind the photo frames. But no one taught us to clean our minds. Not in school. Not at home. Not even in the polished MBA classrooms with their high-gloss slides on "leadership."

We were taught to speak English, not our emotions.

What's Inside the Mental Backpack?

Every morning, professionals like Aman wear invisible backpacks—loaded with cognitive clutter and emotional toxicity. This is not dramatic. It is subtle. A snap at a colleague. A delayed reply to a simple mail. A reluctance to raise a hand in meetings. Symptoms, not of incompetence—but inner overload.

Here's what's worse: we normalize it.

We mistake mental sharpness for mental health. We keep going. We burn out silently—like a candle that does not complain, only shrinks.

And culturally? We are wired to "adjust." Respect elders. Do not question seniors. Maintain harmony. It is a beautiful trait. But in boardrooms, it turns dangerous. People do not raise objections. Ideas go unchallenged. Conflicts stay unresolved, fermenting quietly, corroding clarity.

The Cost of Mental Clutter

Radha, a junior analyst. She disagrees with her manager but remains quiet. Not because she lacks courage—but because she's been told, since childhood, that silence is golden. That moment of suppression multiplies. Soon, she stops sharing at all.

What did the company lose?

Not just Radha's voice—but her vision.

When workplaces ignore emotional hygiene, they pay a hidden tax on creativity, collaboration, and trust. We do not need more dashboards. We need more dialogues. Less posturing, more pause.

Because here's what no one tells you: Your mind is your real workspace. If it is messy, everything else—your logic, your empathy, your performance—pauses.

We Service Cars. Why Not Minds?

You take your car for servicing. You clean your desk. You charge your phone.

But what about your mind?

When did you last reflect on a stubborn emotion? When did you update your mental software—delete a belief that no longer serves you?

5.2 Cleaning mental desktops: practices from cognitive psychology and Eastern philosophy

Let us borrow from two opposite worlds—cognitive psychology and Eastern philosophy. Strangely, they both point to the same practices.

A. Cognitive Psychology: Mental Clarity is Not a Luxury

Let us get real for a second.

We all know that one colleague whose desk is spotless. Color-coded post-its. Mouse aligned with the keyboard. Laptop screen cleaned with more dedication than some people clean their bathrooms.

But what about their mind?

Messy. Cluttered. Overloaded like a Mumbai local at peak hour.

And honestly, most of us aren't very different.

Our calendars are full. Inboxes have red dots screaming for attention. We are toggling between tabs like some kind of corporate DJ. But inside our heads? Chaos. Emotional junk, mental loops, unfinished conversations, insecurities, regrets—all jumbled up in one never-ending traffic jam.

Welcome to the most ignored area of the corporate world: **mental hygiene**.

Let's meet Aman.

Mid-thirties. Works in a tech company in Bangalore. Lives in Whitefield. Drives a white Creta. Has a toddler son who screams "Papa!" every time he comes home. On paper, he's doing well.

But ask Aman how he *feels*, and he'll probably shrug. "Busy yaar. Same old."

What he will not tell you is this:

- He is still upset about a tense call with a client three days ago.
- He is unsure about the feedback he gave to his teammate.
- He did not sleep well because of a nagging fear about that performance review next month.

And that is the thing. Nobody talks about what's really going on *inside*. We talk about deadlines, KPIs, OKRs... but not emotions. Not how we carry yesterday's baggage into today's meetings.

We say, "Be professional."

Translation? "Ignore your feelings."

And in that process, we've turned workplaces into emotionally constipated zones.

The Real Virus: Mental Overload

Think about it. When our laptops hang, we restart them. When our phones slow down, we clear the cache. But what do we do when our mind gets overloaded?

We ignore it. Pretend it is fine. Push through. Add another Red Bull.

Here is the catch: the human brain does not work like a machine. It stores everything—every insult, every self-doubt, every 'What if I mess up?' thought. And when it gets too full, we stop functioning. Not in an obvious way. But in tiny, silent ways:

- You snap at someone without reason.
- You zone out in meetings.
- You avoid difficult conversations.
- You start doubting your own worth.

Welcome to the intellectual clutter.

The Emotional Toxin No One Talks About

Now add emotions to the mix.

You've got suppressed anger, fear of failure, imposter syndrome, jealousy, guilt, and 30 other unnamed feelings floating around like toxic gas. No exit. No release.

In Indian offices, it is even worse. We are told not to question seniors. Not to "create a scene." So people smile on the outside and silently suffer on the inside.

One disagreement with your boss, and you stop speaking up for weeks. One sarcastic comment in a team call, and your motivation quietly dies.

And then managers wonder, "Why is not the team innovative anymore?"

Because people are surviving, not thriving. They're walking around with mental and emotional landmines. And every little thing sets off a blast.

The Need for Mental Housekeeping

You do Diwali cleaning at home, right? Remove cobwebs. Dust the fans. Get rid of useless stuff.

How often do you do that in your *head*?

Just like physical hygiene, mental hygiene needs regular maintenance. But we never learned this in school. Not in college. And not in our fancy MBA programs.

But here's a hack I've seen work in a Pune-based IT firm.

They started something called "Emotional Inbox Zero." Every Friday, 15 minutes. That is it.

No agenda. Just one question: "What's on your mind?"

People spoke. Slowly at first. Then openly.

"I felt dismissed during the meeting."

"I am struggling with personal stuff."

"I am burned out."

No advice. No judgement. Just *listening*. Like a verbal detox.

Within a month, something shifted. People started smiling more. Collaboration improved. Attrition dropped. No rocket science—just less emotional weight.

So, Why Don't More Companies Do This?

Because we still think emotions are "soft."

Let me break this myth.

Emotions run the show. Every business decision, every conflict, every innovation—you name it—it is influenced by what people *feel*, not just what they *think*.

Google ran a huge study called Project Aristotle. You know what made teams successful?

Not IQ. Not degrees. Not crazy productivity.

It was psychological safety—the feeling that you can speak your mind without fear of looking stupid.

If we do not create that space, we'll keep losing good people. Not because they weren't good enough. But because we never gave them space to breathe.

Clean Mind, Clear Vision

So, here's my take.

Mental hygiene is not some Zen monk philosophy. It is practical, urgent, and non-negotiable.

We clean our inbox. We clear our desk. We delete junk files.

Let's start doing the same for our minds.

Every emotion you suppress today will cost you performance tomorrow. Every unprocessed feeling is a tab left open. Too many tabs? The system crashes.

You want to build a great company?

Do not just focus on dashboards and revenue charts.

Start with this simple question:

"How clean is the collective mind of your team?"

Because when the mind is clean, decisions become clear. Energy flows freely. And your team? They will not just work harder. They will work *happier*.

B. Eastern Philosophy: The Mind as a Sacred Space

In Western organizational theories, the mind is often approached as a machine—something to be optimized, debugged, and programmed for performance. We seek productivity hacks, attention-management techniques, and neuropsychological tweaks to boost cognitive efficiency. While useful, this mechanistic view is limited. It risks reducing the human to a tool, ignoring the layered complexity of our inner life.

In contrast, Indian philosophy, especially as seen in traditions like Vedanta, Vipassana, and Yogic psychology, conceptualizes the mind not as a machine but as a field—a kṣhetra, as described in the Bhagavad Gita. This field is productive, dynamic, and multidimensional. It has the capacity to grow weeds, bear fruit, and lie idle. But like any field, it requires cultivation—through practices of discernment, discipline, and silence.

Let us examine three foundational Indian practices that carry deep relevance for modern leadership and organizational development:

1. **Neti-Neti (Not this, not this): Cultivating Detachment from Role-based Identity**

   The practice of **Neti-Neti** is a process of meditative negation. It teaches the aspirant to peel away false layers of self-identification—by repeatedly saying "this is not me," "this is not mine," "I am not this." While this may appear abstract or mysterious, it holds deep practical relevance in a professional context.

   In the corporate arena, especially in hierarchical systems, individuals begin to merge their self-worth with their job titles. A "Senior Manager" starts to believe they are the designation. A "CXO" cannot see life beyond the business card. Promotions feel like personal validation, and performance reviews become emotional verdicts.

   This is where Neti-Neti acts as a powerful antidote. It trains the mind to see roles as functions, not identities. It allows the individual to perform with detachment—not indifference, but a conscious separation between who they are and what they do.

   When practiced regularly, Neti-Neti builds resilience against ego inflation and emotional reactivity. Leaders become more open to feedback, less threatened by dissent, and more capable of promoting psychological safety in teams. The ego, which often clouds decision-making, becomes more transparent—less of a master, more of a servant.

2. **Pranayama (Breath Discipline): Regulating Emotion, Enhancing Cognition**

   The ancient yogis knew what modern neuroscientists are now confirming—the breath is the bridge between the body and the mind. In high-stress environments, the first casualty is breathing. We unconsciously shift to shallow, rapid breaths, which signal the brain to trigger survival-mode responses: anxiety, tunnel vision, impatience.

   Pranayama, the systematic control of breath, is not merely a wellness tool—it is a thought regulator. Practices such as Nadi Shodhana (alternate nostril breathing) or Bhramari (humming breath) directly influence the autonomic nervous system. They reduce cortisol levels, enhance vagal tone, and improve attentional control.

   What this means for organizations is impactful. Executives trained in breath awareness exhibit lower burnout, sharper decision-making, and greater emotional composure during conflicts or crises. A COO who begins the day with 10 minutes of breathwork is statistically more likely to conduct a calmer negotiation or deliver feedback without aggression.

   Pranayama therefore, becomes a leadership enabler, not a relaxation technique. It is similar to tuning an instrument before performance—not an accessory, but a prerequisite.

3. **Antar Mouna (Inner Silence): Witnessing Without Judgement**

   In our hyper-verbal workplaces, silence is often mistaken for disengagement. But in the Indian meditative tradition, silence is not the absence of speech—it is the presence of inner observation. The practice of Antar Mouna, or inner silence, is about sitting with one's thoughts without identifying with them. You do not suppress the thoughts; you observe them rise and fall like waves.

This ability to witness without judgment is crucial in leadership. A manager who can observe their anger without acting on it will be more ethical and empathetic. A team leader who can hold space for diverse opinions without rushing to assert their own will improve inclusiveness.

Organizations that encourage reflective practices are not indulging in "soft skills"; they are investing in mindful leadership development. Over time, such practices reduce the emotional charge behind mental narratives—"I am not good enough," "They do not respect me," "I must prove myself." As these internal dialogues lose their sting, what develops is clarity, composure, and genuine listening.

5.3 From Wellness to Wisdom: Reframing Corporate Mindfulness

Progressive firms—Infosys, Wipro, HCL, Dell, IBM, HPand even select PSUs—have introduced corporate yoga and mindfulness programs. But these are still often framed as "wellness perks," packaged between Friday pizza parties and weekend outbound retreats. The underlying philosophy gets diluted, and the practices are seen as optional or ornamental.

What is urgently needed is a reframing—from wellness to leadership capability. Neti-Neti is not just spiritual—it is a tool for ego management. Pranayama is not just relaxing—it sharpens executive function. Antar Mouna is not passive—it trains attention and emotional intelligence.

When Indian philosophy is applied not as a view, but as inner technology, it builds organizations that are not only resourceful but also ethical, compassionate, and resilient.

This is not a return to tradition for the sake of nostalgia. It is a strategic alignment with India's strengths. As global leadership models begin to question the costs of burnout, toxic competitiveness, and emotional suppression, India could lead not just in tech or economics, but in the art of self-mastery.

For leaders willing to look inward, the field of the mind awaits cultivation. The storm of fear and ego can be cleared. The seeds of insight and stillness can be sown. And from this well-tended field, a new kind of leadership can rise—one that thrives not on power, but on presence.

Leaders as Custodians of Mental Hygiene

For far too long, Indian corporate leadership has been influenced—almost colonized—by Western theories of efficiency, goal-orientation, and hierarchical control. The leader is positioned as the driver, the taskmaster, the strategist with KPIs etched in stone. Meetings begin with timelines and end with trackers. Even the most well-meaning managers are often reduced to deadline monitors, asking in their weekly sync-ups, "Are we done yet?" or "How far are we from the milestone?"

But the 21st-century workplace, particularly in post-pandemic India, has undergone an unspoken transformation. Employees today are not just units of productivity; they are individuals dealing with chronic stress, digital overload, and emotional fragmentation. The real question is no longer "Are you done?", but "How are you coping?"

It is in this evolving ecosystem that leaders must shift—from being mere goal-setters to space-holders.

This idea may seem subtle, even intangible, but its consequences are significant.

The Case of Nayana: Redesigning the Managerial Lens

Consider the example of Nayana, a mid-level manager in a Mumbai-based services firm. Faced with high attrition and team disengagement, she introduced a small but radical ritual: "Mind Check" Mondays. It was not a performance dashboard, or a project debrief, but a human check-in. Each team member was asked to share one word that described their mental or emotional state at that moment.

Initially, the team was sceptical. Some thought it was HR-driven. Others feared it would devolve into therapy sessions or sentimentality. But slowly, the vocabulary began to evolve. Words like "drained," "anxious," "hopeful," and "motivated" started emerging. These weren't metrics that could be plotted on a spreadsheet. They were signals—honest, raw, and revealing.

Nayana did not interrupt or solve. She just listened. And she held the space—not to fix, but to witness.

Over time, this small window of psychological safety led to deeper conversations. The team began reassigning tasks not just based on skill or hierarchy but based on emotional bandwidth. If someone was overwhelmed, others stepped in. If someone was energised, they volunteered to take more. Productivity did not fall—it stabilised. Burnout decreased. Resignations slowed. Morale climbed.

What Nayana had done, perhaps without even realising it, was transform leadership from task management to **emotional stewardship**.

Leadership as Emotional Infrastructure

This shift is not a soft skill—it is strategic infrastructure for future-ready organizations.

Modern Indian workplaces, especially in tech, services, and startups, are characterized by hyper-responsiveness. Employees toggle between MS Teams, Slack, Zoom, Jira, and emails—all while trying to meet customer expectations in real time. In such a setting, what breaks first is not competence, but emotional continuity. The human brain was not designed to juggle 20 priorities without a break. Anxiety, decision fatigue, and motivational loss soon follow.

Yet, our leadership metrics remain traditional on lagging indicators like productivity and targets, rather than leading indicators like emotional energy, focus, and mental resilience.

Here is where Indian philosophical wisdom can be a powerful complement. Indian tradition—particularly in Ayurveda, Yogic

Psychology, and the Gita—emphasizes the interior condition of the individual. True karma, as per the Gita, is about alignment, not just action. Leadership, then, must concern itself not only with outcomes, but with inner clarity—of both the leader and the team.

When leaders evolve into space-holders, they create an environment where individuals can surface their truths without fear of judgment. This is not indulgent; it is intelligent. A psychologically safe environment leads to better risk-taking, faster problem resolution, and stronger team cohesion—as shown in multiple studies by organizations like Google (Project Aristotle).

The Myth of Time Management: It is About Attention and Meaning

One of the most persistent myths in corporate culture is that time is the most critical resource. Countless leadership workshops teach us to schedule better, prioritize smarter, and eliminate distractions. But deeper research and lived experience reveal that attention—not time—is the important resource.

You can give someone eight uninterrupted hours, but if their mind is preoccupied, emotionally burdened, or existentially numb, output will be compromised.

Good leaders, therefore, are not those who maximize the calendar. They are those who optimize attention, regulate emotion, and co-create meaning.

From Transaction to Transformation

At its core, this shift in leadership is about moving from transaction to transformation. Task completion, while necessary, is no longer sufficient. Leaders must now steward states of mind, spaces of trust, and cultures of care.

The Indian workplace is not just a site of economic activity—it is a small-scale version of societal change. Gender dynamics, generational divides, and class transitions play out subtly but powerfully in our teams. A manager's ability to listen without judging, lead without dominating, and nurture without rescuing becomes not just a managerial skill—but a civic one.

Perhaps the most powerful thing a leader can say in the corporate world is not "Let's push harder," but: "Let's pause. Let's breathe. And let's begin again—with awareness."

5.4 Rituals That Matter — Practical Implementations

Over the decades, I have seen organizations that succeeded not just because of their strategic brilliance but because they made room—intentionally or otherwise—for quiet rituals that cleared the mind, settled emotions, and sharpened perspective. These are not always large-scale initiatives. In fact, the most transformative changes often come from small, repeated practices that support psychological clarity and collective trust.

Let me share six such rituals that any team or leader can implement—not as policies, but as cultural habits. Think of them as emotional housekeeping. Or, if you prefer a more Indian analogy, these are like the simple yogic stretches you do every morning to ensure your day begins well—not flashy but deeply sustaining.

1. Mental Stand-Downs: A Pause with No Purpose

In most organizations, time is a precious commodity. Meetings are structured with tight agendas, KPIs, and follow-ups. But every now and then, we need to gift ourselves an hour with no agenda. I call this the *Mental Stand-Down.*

Once a month, teams should meet for an hour—not to brainstorm or execute—but to simply reflect and share. The format is simple. People sit together in silence for ten minutes and jot down what's been weighing on their minds—professionally or personally. Then, whoever feels comfortable shares.

One engineering team I knew at a manufacturing firm in Mysore tried this once. It felt awkward at first. But by the third session, people began to open up. A quiet colleague spoke about feeling left out of decisions. Another spoke about sleeplessness due to uncertainty in his role. No decisions were made in that hour, but something shifted—the air became lighter. People listened better, spoke softer.

We underestimate the power of collective silence and voluntary openness.

2. Decision Audit Logs: Looking Back with Clarity

After major decisions—product or service launches, hiring choices, budget reallocations—most teams move on quickly. The next fire needs attention. But if we never pause to relook at our thinking, we become prisoners of unseen biases.

The *Decision Audit Log* is a simple ritual: after every major decision, take ten minutes to ask the team three questions:

- What assumptions did we make?
- What fears or desires might have influenced our judgment?
- Would we make the same decision again if we had to do it today?

This is not about blame. It is about building decision literacy. I recall a senior leader at a telecom company who began doing this after vendor selections. Over a year, his team discovered that many choices were subtly biased by "availability bias"—the tendency to favour options that were easier to access rather than better in value. The ritual did not just clean up decisions—it elevated the quality of thinking.

3. Digital Pause: Silence in a Noisy World

The modern workplace is drenched in noise—pings, calls, updates, notifications. It is the corporate version of standing in the middle of a traffic junction with no traffic lights.

Enter the *Digital Pause*—an afternoon every week when emails are paused, meetings are frozen, and employees are free to focus on deep work or mindful rest.

A tech startup in Bengaluru tested this concept every Wednesday afternoon. Initially, leadership worried about lost productivity, but the results spoke for themselves. Within weeks, engineers produced higher-quality code with fewer errors, collaboration became more intentional, and employee satisfaction scores rose. Even customer support metrics improved, as reps returned to work with renewed clarity and patience. The unexpected upside? The team became more knowledgeable overall, proving that constant connectivity does not equal productivity—focused time does.

Silence is not a luxury; it is a necessity, especially in knowledge-driven industries. The Digital Pause is a reminder that in an era of hyper-stimulation, businesses must deliberately create space for reflection. By resisting the cult of busyness, companies can encourage sharper thinking, innovation, and sustainable performance. The question is not whether organizations can afford to pause—it is whether they can afford not to.

4. Thought Swaps: The Anonymous Listening Post

In the Indian workplace, hierarchy often makes it difficult to speak freely. People self-censor. They avoid conflict. But that does not mean thoughts disappear. They just sink below the surface, waiting to erupt in passive resistance or disengagement.

A Thought Swap is a simple yet powerful practice where a digital or physical board is made available to all team members, encouraging them to anonymously share their inner state under three thoughtful categories: Worries (concerns they're carrying), Wins (moments of personal or team success), and Wisdom (learnings, reflections, or insights). This open, non-judgmental space brings psychological safety, emotional expression, and shared learning—building a culture of empathy, trust, and collective intelligence within the organization.

At a mid-sized logistics firm in Pune, one such board revealed that junior staff felt excluded from innovation discussions. Another person anonymously praised a peer's empathy during a crisis. Over time, the board became a place for emotional detox and cross-pollination of insight.

When people see their thoughts valued—even anonymously—they feel seen.

5.5 The Paradox of Performance

Here's the final insight. Many organizations, especially in the Indian context, still regard emotional hygiene as a soft skill — something that is desirable but dispensable. It is often grouped with weekend yoga sessions, motivational posters, or HR-led well-being drives. But what if this categorization itself is the problem? What if, instead of treating it as peripheral, we began to treat emotional hygiene as the very architecture of wise decision-making?

Our thoughts are often shadows cast by emotions — worry, bias, fear, anticipation, and pride. Corrupts judgment, misdirects attention, and creates a fog in which poor decisions are made.

Let me explain with an example from my own career. During my stint at a multinational, we were once evaluating a joint venture proposal with a global technology giant. The numbers made sense. The market potential was obvious. But during one internal meeting, a mid-level manager shared a subtle, emotionally driven concern. He said, "Sir, I just do not feel comfortable with the aggression of their team. It reminded me of a past deal that became very transactional."

Now, in many corporate settings, such a remark might have been brushed aside as 'subjective.' But we took it seriously. We paused the evaluation and initiated a culture compatibility study. Six weeks later, the study confirmed what the gut had warned: our values clashed on people development, long-term vision, and customer handling. The deal was dropped. The emotional whisper had saved us from a strategic misstep.

Why do I recount this? Because it underscores that emotion is not the opposite of logic — it is the soil in which logic either roots or rots. And if the soil is contaminated with unresolved stress, fatigue, resentment, or anxiety, even the most brilliant strategies falter.

In offices, the challenge is doubly complex. We have inherited the residues of colonial bureaucracy, where hierarchy often suppresses honest emotional expression. At the same time, we have embraced Silicon Valley urgency, where speed often replaces reflection. The result? A workplace culture where people keep pushing.

Pushing through confusion. Pushing despite exhaustion. Pushing away inner conflict. As if performance were a treadmill that punished any pause.

But high performance, as I have learned through two decades across sectors, is not about pushing harder. It is about cleaning clearly. Cleaning the mind of mental clutter. Clearing unprocessed emotion. Clarifying intent before rushing into action. That is emotional hygiene.

Let us not get distracted by the word 'emotional', and this is about soft couches and deep breathing. No. Emotional hygiene is as operationally relevant as cost control or market segmentation. Think of it as maintaining the cleanliness of the cognitive lens through which all business judgment is made.

This is not a fantasy. It is very much possible.

From Hygiene to Insight.

A typical Monday morning meeting in any company. The agenda is clear: project updates, revenue targets, client escalations. Now think of a different version of that meeting. One where the first five minutes are spent not in PowerPoint, but in silence. Intentional silence. A moment for everyone to settle, breathe, and enter the room not just with their laptops, but with their presence.

Then, before diving into deliverables, the team is asked a question: "What emotional state do we want to end this week with?" Words like 'energized', 'balanced', 'collaborative', or 'respected' are voiced. These become anchors. Reminders. A way to return to the 'why' when the 'what' becomes overwhelming.

That is what I mean by tending to the hygiene of the mind. Meetings stop being updates and become insights. Work stops being a checklist and becomes a journey.

Silence, once feared as awkward, becomes sacred. Not because it is exotic, but because it creates space for reflection. And in reflection, insight is born. As the Bhagavad Gita says, "Yoga is the journey of the self, through the self, to the self." Leadership, too, is such a journey. And it demands space, silence, and hygiene.

So the next time you see a colleague hunched over their laptop, brows furrowed, energy distressed, do not just ask, "What do you need to finish?" Ask, "What do you need to clear?" Because clarity is not merely the absence of confusion. It is the presence of perspective.

And perspective arises when the emotional noise is cleared, like fog lifting from a mountain path.

In one of my mentoring sessions with a young leader from Hyderabad, I suggested she introduce a 10-minute 'clarity check-in' with her team every Friday. It was simple. Three questions: What went well? What drained you? What are you learning about yourself?

She called me a month later. "Sir," she said, "my team is now having conversations they never had in four years. We are not just working better; we are understanding each other better."

That is the power of emotional hygiene. It is not a cost. It is an investment. An investment in clarity. In insight. In trust. And ultimately, in wisdom.

To all leaders reading this, I leave you with this: You are not just custodians of results. You are custodians of environments. And environments do not just run on metrics. They run on emotional clarity.

So, before you design the next strategy offsite, think also of designing a strategy for emotional hygiene. Because in my experience, the cleanest minds make the wisest moves.

And wise moves are the only sustainable competitive advantage in a world that is noisy, fast, and emotionally fragmented.

Let this be your organization's mantra:

Declutter the mind. Disarm the emotion. Discover the meaning.

Not just for productivity.

But for peace.

The Calm Catalyst Truth #5:

"Clean minds do not just think better—they lead better. Emotional clarity is not a luxury; it is the quiet engine of good judgment, wise decisions, and sustainable performance."

CHAPTER 6

THE SILENT LEADERS: CATALYSTS IN THE MIDDLE

6.1 Recognizing Quiet Influencers and Hidden Changemakers

"The Deck Was Right, But the Voice Was not"

Arjun was one of those team members you would never see scrambling. Calm in the storm, quiet during meetings, and meticulous in his work. His decks were solid, his insights sharp. But there was one place where things always went sideways—**presentations**.

It was not because Arjun lacked confidence. Or clarity. Or communication skills.

It was something subtler.

The week before every big client review, Arjun would prepare with sincerity. He knew his stuff—numbers, logic, flow. But the moment he ran it by his manager, things changed.

"Do not open with that graph," his manager would say.

"You need to use more buzzwords. Make it crisp."

"This style feels too dry."

"Be more assertive. I would do it like this…"

None of it was mean-spirited. His manager, in fact, meant well. He was a seasoned presenter, charismatic, assertive—the kind who could command a room even before the deck was up. But what he did not realize was this: he was giving feedback not to improve the message, but to reshape it in his own image.

What followed was a quiet, dull moment.

Arjun would go back, adjust slides, tweak the tone, and re-record his notes. Each time, he became a little less certain—not of the content, but of himself.

By the time the final version was ready, it was no longer his voice on that deck. It was a stitched version of expectations.

And every time he stood to present, he felt disconnected. Robotic. Measured.

Not nervous—just unaligned.

The client smiled, the feedback was "good," but Arjun knew it could have been great—if he had spoken his own language.

The Hidden Cost of Standardization

We often assume team members fear public speaking because of performance anxiety.

But more often, it is **approval anxiety**.

They fear not the audience, but the pre-judgment from their own managers.

And here is the kicker: feedback, when framed poorly, does not just change the presentation.

It rewrites the presenter.

What many leaders miss is this—there's a difference between improving quality and enforcing conformity. And in trying to make presentations "professional," "polished," or "our standard," they unknowingly mute the very originality that could have made it resonate.

The Micro-Shift

One day, Arjun's new director overheard part of a review.

Later, she stopped by and said,

"You know, I saw your raw draft earlier—it had heart. Why don't you present the way that feels natural to you? You have earned the room. Let's see *you*."

That sentence changed everything.

Arjun walked into the next review with the same deck—but with his own rhythm. He did not overemphasize. He paused when he felt like it. He told a story to explain a metric. He made space for silence and was able to accommodate some of his managers' suggestions too.

And for the first time in months, he saw nods, real ones.

The client smiled—not out of courtesy, but interest.

That day, something clicked.

He was not just presenting. He was leading the narrative.

Insight: Authenticity is not a Style. It's a Signal.

In high-performance environments, the temptation to standardize is high. Managers want consistency, polish, and reliability.

But leadership is not about copy-pasting charisma.

It is about creating space where people can present their ideas in their own voice. Especially for calm, thoughtful, introverted team members—whose style may not be loud but is just as powerful. Because when people present from alignment, they don't just deliver.

They connect!!

In every workplace, between the declarations of top leadership and the tireless commitment of frontline workers, exists a domination often covered from formal recognition—the space occupied by middle managers and individual contributors who quietly yet thoughtfully shape the character of an organization. They are rarely celebrated in keynote addresses or featured in glossy annual reports. Yet, it is through their daily choices, their consistent presence, and their deep emotional attachment that the culture of a company is either reinforced or reimagined.

These are the *Unspoken Leaders*. Not by rank or title, but by impact. They do not flash credentials or command rooms with heroism. Instead, they lead with presence, with intuition, and with a kind of leadership that is harder to quantify but deeply felt. Their leadership is not a role they play—it is an essence they carry.

Take, for instance, Ananya, a mid-level operations manager at a bustling technology firm in Hyderabad. She did not have the appeal of a charismatic speaker, nor did she seek visibility in town halls. What she had was something far more valuable—emotional resonance. Over five quiet years, Ananya became the silent anchor of her department. Her desk was not the biggest, her team not the largest, but her impact far exceeded her pay grade.

Her juniors stayed longer not because they had to, but because they *wanted* to. They volunteered for stretch assignments, not for brownie points, but out of a sense of shared responsibility. This was not accidental—it was nurtured. Ananya created a space where trust was not enforced; it was naturally grown. She noticed when someone was unusually quiet. She always asked, "Is everything okay?"—and meant it. She made room for half-baked ideas without laughing them off. And when pressure rolled downhill from senior leadership, she absorbed its weight rather than passing it on like a hot coal.

She did not wear leadership like a badge. She wore it like skin—natural, constant, and unnoticed unless you really paid attention. That is the hallmark of The Unspoken Calm leadership—it works best when it is invisible.

Ananya never appeared in the quarterly leadership shout-outs. But something remarkable happened. Her language started showing up in others' speech. "As Ananya always says…" became a preamble in meetings she did not attend. People who had worked under her started managing their own teams with similar grace. Her influence moved not through authority, but through atmosphere. Her leadership was not institutionalized, but it was internalized.

This is the paradox of mid-tier leadership. They do not wield the authority to redefine corporate strategy. They cannot change compensation structures or redefine market positioning. But they hold something more intimate and deeper—the power to influence how people *feel* in the workplace. And that power is both radical and rare.

In a world obsessed with dashboards and KPIs, these leaders work in the invisible layers—the emotional data, the behavioural patterns, the unseen forces that drive motivation and belonging. They act as cultural thermostats. When stress rises, they cool the room. When teams drift, they bring them together. They manage not just workflows, but the *flow* itself—the energy between people, the friction that erodes trust, and the sparks that ignite creativity.

They reduce noise without demanding attention. They make others shine while standing in the shadows. And in doing so, they build what we often forget to measure—the emotional infrastructure of an organization.

One might claim that simply organizing birthday celebrations or anniversary events can help boost morale. But the Unspoken Leaders know better. They understand that celebration without connection is hollow. That an event on a calendar means little unless people feel remembered, respected, and real in that moment. Ananya never made a show of such celebrations, but when she brought a homemade cake for a junior team member who had just moved to the city, it resonated deeper than any HR-sponsored cupcakes ever could.

Her leadership was not performative; it was personal. And that is why it was powerful.

Organizations often talk about transformation as if it begins at the top and trickles down. But real, sustained change often germinates in the middle—where strategy meets execution, where pressure meets empathy, and where policies must pass through people to become practice. The silent leaders operate here, in this messy and magical middle ground.

And in a world that often confuses leadership with visibility, they remind us of a timeless truth: *Presence is power, even when it whispers.*

6.2 How Middle Managers and Individual Contributors Shape Culture Under the Radar

The Myth of the Spotlight Leader

Leadership development programs have a predictable obsession—high potentials, charismatic visionaries, and C-suite executives. They are groomed, spotlighted, and celebrated. But what if the real architects of transformation are the ones operating in the shadows?

Mid-level managers, individual contributors, and quiet performers are the soil where change takes root. They move through organizations with an intuitive sense of timing—knowing when to push, when to pause, when to speak, and when to listen. Their leadership is not loud, it is felt.

A fintech startup in Bengaluru. A product designer named Arvind—no fancy title, no executive mandate—decides to host fortnightly "design retrospectives." No one asked him to. No one expected it. He simply invites his colleagues to reflect: *What worked? What* did not*? What could we do better?*

At first, only a handful showed up. But slowly, something shifted. Engineers started joining. Marketers dropped in. Even interns lingered. These weren't just meetings—they became sacred spaces where pixels and user journeys gave way to something deeper: pride in craft, cross-team listening, and creative vulnerability.

All because one person asked: *"What can we learn together?"*

Influence Without Authority—The New Leadership Currency

What does Arvind's story teach us?

Modern influence is not hierarchical. It is atmospheric.

It does not spread through org charts or job titles. It moves through stories, symbols, and shared emotional experiences. The quiet leaders—the ones who do not demand attention but command respect—do not *push* culture. They breathe it.

Yet, here is the tragedy:

Their contributions remain invisible to formal appraisal systems.

- The manager who mediates conflicts quietly, ensuring a team stays productive, has no KPI for "prevented dysfunction."

- The analyst who notices early signs of burnout in peers and quietly redistributes workloads gets no bonus for "saved attrition."
- The customer support rep whose calm presence reassures an angry client is not lauded for "emotional labour."

But these acts—small, unseen—are what hold organizations together.

The Cost of Confusing Visibility with Value

We live in an era that equates noise with impact. If you're not presenting in boardrooms, posting on LinkedIn, or leading high-profile initiatives, do you even matter?

Yes. More than you know.

Silent leaders:

- Stabilize teams during chaos.
- Spot fractures before they become breaks.
- Sustain morale when motivation flickers.

But because their work is not flashy, it is dismissed as "just part of the job." Meanwhile, the loudest voices—often the least effective—get promoted.

This is not just unfair. It is unsustainable.

Organizations that fail to recognize quiet leadership are essentially burning their own foundations.

6.3 The Quiet Revolution

The future belongs to organizations that see the unseen—the quiet forces shaping culture where no one is looking. Because real change is not crafted in keynote speeches or polished mission statements. It happens in small rooms, in unscripted moments, in the daily choices no one applauds—the extra minute taken to listen, the unasked-for help, the refusal to cut corners when no one's watching.

It is built by the Arvind's of the world—the ones who lead without permission, without titles, without fanfare. They do not wait for a spotlight; they carry their own light. They fix what is broken before it shatters. They speak truths others avoid. They show up, steady and unshaken, in the storms everyone else races to escape.

Yet too often, they remain invisible to systems that mistake volume for value, charisma for competence.

It is time we start noticing them.

Not with empty praise, but with real recognition—promotions, influence, and the power to shape what comes next. Because when we finally learn to honour the quiet builders, we will not just change workplaces.

We will change the world.

The Need for a Leadership Paradigm Shift

In her workshops, Sibel Terhaar often reminds us that leadership is not a spotlight—it is a constellation. Each star, no matter how faint, contributes to the illumination of the night. The brilliance of an organization does not come from one radiant sun at the top but from a sky of interconnected lights that support, respond, and reflect. In this metaphor, silent leaders are not outliers. They are the guiding stars that quietly set direction, hold emotional space, and bring reason to the chaos.

We must shift how we recognize leadership. Traditional models reward those who are loudest, fastest, and most visible. But what if the real power lies in those who slow down enough to listen deeply, who ask questions that reveal unspoken truths, and who stabilize rather than steer? These are not hypothetical traits. They are observable realities in middle managers and individual contributors across the globe.

Organizations must move from measurement to meaning. Quantitative KPIs alone cannot capture the nuanced ways in which culture is built and resilience is sustained. We need feedback systems that capture how someone made others feel—how they resolved tensions, mentored quietly, or simply made work feel safe. Instead of only tracking metrics, let's also measure moments. Instead of appraising outputs, let's acknowledge outcomes that are emotional, human, and long-term.

Now think of a peer-nominated system for "Everyday Leadership Moments"—not for highest sales or fastest project closures, but for kindness under pressure, for mentoring without mandate, for maintaining morale in moments of uncertainty. These recognitions do not just boost individual morale; they shape organizational DNA. They remind everyone that values are not theoretical—they are practiced.

And what about learning? Most corporate leadership programs focus on competencies and simulations. What if we invited storytelling? What if people shared real accounts of moments that tested their character or challenged their ethics? Storytelling circles are not just warm and fuzzy—they are the main tools of alignment. They surface the invisible. They democratize voice. They inspire by example, not position.

There is much the C-suite can learn from the middle:

- Presence Over Performance: Silent leaders reveal that the most impactful presence often comes from those who are calm, observant, and steady.
- Stability in Ambiguity: In times of flux, it is the mid-layer that holds the emotional temperature of the organization. Their steadiness becomes the silent scaffolding of success.
- Empathy as Efficiency: Efficiency is not always speed. Sometimes, it is listening carefully enough to avoid missteps, burnout, or disengagement.
- Culture in Micro-Moments: Culture is not an off-site exercise. It is built into how people respond to setbacks, how feedback is given, and how inclusion is practiced on the ground.

Senior leaders must step out of thought and into action. They must notice who keeps teams together during transitions, who sets the tone without needing a title, and who lives the company's values without broadcasting them. These individuals are not aspiring to lead—they already are.

In the end, perhaps the boldest thing a leader can do is to make room for others to lead quietly. In a world obsessed with charisma, may we rediscover the elegance of consistency. In a world that celebrates individual wins, may we return to collective wisdom. And in organizations that often echo with noise, may we learn to hear the power of the still, small voice.

As we step into a time defined by artificial intelligence, hybrid structures, and fluid roles, traditional leadership constructs will inevitably shift. Loudness will lose its edge. Titles will lose their gravity. Hierarchies will dissolve into networks. In this world, the most valuable leadership asset will be the ability to hold space for others—with wisdom, steadiness, and grace.

These calm catalysts do not announce their arrival. They do not campaign for attention. Yet, they change cultures, one gesture at a time. They build emotional infrastructure that holds teams together during change. They restore the soul of the workplace.

And often, it is in the quietest corners that the strongest foundations are laid. Let us not miss them. Let us learn to listen. Let us choose to follow them.

The Calm Catalyst Truth #6:

"True leadership is not a title worn but a presence felt. In the middle of the hierarchy lies the pulse of the organization—quietly steadying the chaos, silently shaping the culture."

PART III

DESIGNING FOR DEPTH AND DYNAMISM

CHAPTER 7

CULTURE CODES: EMBEDDING ENERGY, EMPATHY, AND ETHICS

7.1 Designing Organizations to Respect the Invisible

In the heart of a small village in Karnataka, there was a temple with no idol. People came there not to offer prayers to a visible deity, but to experience a sense of peace and quiet. The villagers believed that the divine did not need form to be felt. The spirit of the temple was its silence, its cleanliness, and the sense of being welcome.

Much like this temple, the soul of an organization is often invisible. It is not in the quarterly reports, not in the slogans on the walls, and surely not in the dress codes. It is in the unsaid rules, the unspoken respect, the way people smile at the security guard, or how a senior waits for a junior to finish speaking.

This invisible culture is what truly holds an organization together. And yet, it is the most overlooked. We build processes and policies, hire consultants for structure and strategy, but forget to ask—what energy does our workplace give off?

When we talk about designing organizations to respect the invisible, we are really asking: do we acknowledge what cannot be measured? Can we sense what cannot be graphed? Because in this age of data and dashboards, we are losing sight of the very elements that breathe life into our workplaces.

Let's take the example of a small garment factory in Tiruppur. The owner, Rajagopal, is not an MBA graduate. He does not know much about market segmentation. But every morning, before workers begin, he stands at the gate, greets each one by name, and asks about their family. If someone looks tired, he does not ask for productivity metrics—he sends them to rest. Over the years, attrition at his factory has been near zero. No HR strategy can replicate what he built by simply paying attention.

In large corporations, there is a long-standing practice of compartmentalizing—separating the professional from the personal. We are often told to leave our problems at the door, to wear a mask of composure, and to function with mechanical precision regardless of what's unfolding in our personal lives. But this assumption—that people can somehow split themselves in two—is deeply flawed. Humans do not come in boxes neatly labelled "home" and "office." We are one integrated being. When a team member is dealing with anxiety, grief, or personal turmoil, it does not stay behind in their living room. It walks in with them, sits at their desk, and shadows them through every task.

Yet in too many workplaces, this truth is ignored. Performance is prioritized, but presence is not understood. Expectations remain rigid, while humanity is expected to be flexible. And in that silence, people start wearing emotional shield—hiding their struggles, suppressing their needs, and pretending all is well, just to survive another day.

But the moment a leader chooses kindness over protocol, everything begins to change.

Consider a manager who notices a shift in someone's energy and gently asks, "Is everything okay?"—without judgment, without performance consequences. That single question, that simple gesture, can pierce through months of emotional fatigue. It tells the employee: "You matter beyond your output." When a leader acknowledges a person's pain and holds space without trying to fix or evaluate, they become more than a boss—they become a bridge.

A kind leader does not need grand gestures. Just their awareness and permission to be human are enough to create ripples. It normalizes vulnerability, encourages open dialogue, and, most importantly, it builds a culture of psychological safety. And in such cultures, people do not just perform better—they stay longer, collaborate deeper, and lead with more empathy themselves.

Over time, this simple truth becomes clear: compassion is not a detour from productivity—it is the path to it. When people feel seen and safe, they give their best. Not because they're being monitored, but because they're being trusted.

And it all begins with a leader who dares to look beyond deadlines and sees the person behind the role.

Respecting the invisible means learning to value the things we often overlook—time, tone, and temperament. In our corporate environments, the loudest voice in the room often gets the most attention, and the person who replies fastest is considered the sharpest. But true leadership—and true understanding—requires us to look beyond the obvious. Time is not just about deadlines and schedules. It is also about space—allowing others the time to think, reflect, and respond. A pause before answering a question is not always a sign of confusion or hesitation. Sometimes, it is a quiet form of wisdom—someone weighing their words, thinking deeply before they speak, choosing response over reaction.

Similarly, tone matters more than we realize. The same words, spoken gently or harshly, can land in completely different ways. A leader who speaks with calmness and clarity often creates an environment of trust, even in tense moments. On the other hand, a sharp tone—especially when used carelessly—can shut down creativity, cause unwanted fear, and damage relationships. Respecting tone is about being mindful not just of what we say, but how we say it—and how it makes the other person feel.

Then there is temperament—each person's unique rhythm, energy, and emotional makeup. Some are fast-paced and action-driven. Others are slow, steady thinkers. Some thrive in brainstorming sessions; others need quiet time to process before they contribute. Respecting the invisible means understanding these differences without judgment. It means not mistaking introversion for disengagement, or if silence equals indifference.

In fact, some of the most reflective ideas come from those who speak less and observe more. Their quiet presence is not a lack of participation—it is a sign of depth.

Results are measured, and KPIs dominate dashboards; the invisible traits often go unnoticed. But these are the very things that build trust, encourage inclusion, and deepen team connection. When we begin to honour time, tone, and temperament—not just output—we create cultures that don't just perform but persist. To respect the invisible is to value the human. And that is where the soul of any great workplace quietly begins to shine.

To design for the invisible, here are three foundational questions every leader must ask:

1. What do people feel when they walk into this workplace?
    - Is it fear? Or belonging?
    - Do they feel they can be themselves, or must they wear a mask?
2. Who gets interrupted and who gets heard?
    - Are meetings providing opportunities to exchange, or displays of authority?
3. What is celebrated?
    - Only targets? Or also the grace with which failure was handled?

Once these questions are answered honestly, the design can begin. Not on paper, but in behaviour. Start small—change how on boarding is done, make space for silence in meetings, offer gratitude as often as feedback.

True culture is a living presence. Like air, we do not see it—but we breathe it every moment.

7.2 Creating Rituals, Rhythms, and Relational Intelligence

When I was young, my grandmother would light the lamp every evening and place a small tulsi leaf in front of it. This act, simple as it was, brought a sense of rhythm to our day. It was her way of telling us—day is ending, gather yourselves, and breathe. It had nothing to do with religion. It was about presence.

In organizations, rituals serve a similar purpose. They bring predictability, meaning, and grounding. But not all rituals are created. Some develop. Others must be nurtured. And all must serve the purpose of reminding people that they are seen and valued.

Let me tell you about a unique little ritual that quietly transformed the culture of a software company in Kochi. It is called the "Failure Circle," and it happens on the last Friday of every month. It is not part of any official agenda or mandated HR program. There are no slides, no KPIs, and no corporate jargon. Just a group of team members, sitting in a circle, sharing their stories of failure—honest, unfiltered, and from the heart.

It all began, as most meaningful things do, quite by accident. A young developer, just a few months into his job, stood up during a team meeting and admitted that he had made a coding error that set the team back by two days. His voice trembled slightly as he spoke, expecting a reprimand. But instead of reprimanding, his manager simply nodded, smiled, and said, "Thank you for your honesty." Then, to everyone's surprise, the manager shared a mistake he had made ten years earlier—one that had affected an entire client delivery.

That one moment of vulnerability created a wave. People looked at each other differently after that meeting. The young developer was not seen as careless anymore—he was seen as courageous. The manager was not just a boss—he became human. Slowly, the team decided to create space for these stories. And hence, the "Failure Circle" was born.

Each month, someone volunteers to share. It is not compulsory, and there's no pressure to be insightful. Sometimes the stories are small—like forgetting to save a presentation before the laptop crashed. Sometimes they're bigger—like misjudging a client requirement or misunderstanding a teammate. But the beauty lies not in the size of the mistake, but in the honesty with which it is shared and the lesson that comes with it.

The most surprising thing is what happened over time. Teams became more open. People started asking for help earlier. Managers grew more empathetic. And juniors began to see failure not as something to fear, but as something to learn from. It created a culture where trying was more important than getting it right every time.

One senior architect said, "Earlier, we used to wear our success like armour. Now, we carry our failures like teachers." Is it not beautiful?

You see, in a world that celebrates only wins and rewards only outcomes, creating a space where failure is welcomed—without judgment—is revolutionary. It reminds us that behind every smart solution is a trail of unseen errors. And behind every confident professional is a collection of quietly carried failures.

This little ritual in Kochi teaches us something big: when we allow people to be real, we allow them to grow.

What do such rituals achieve? They humanize the workplace. They tell people: here, it is safe to be real.

Rhythms, on the other hand, are the heartbeat of culture. They are not grand events with big banners and buzzwords. They are gentle patterns that repeat with meaning. Like the steady rhythm of a heartbeat, they remind people that something deeper is at work below the surface of day-to-day tasks.

Take, for example, a team that starts its daily stand-up not by jumping into problems and tasks, but with a moment of gratitude. Each person shares one thing they're thankful for—work-related or personal. It might be something small, like "I finally completed that bug fix," or something big, like "My child is recovering well from illness." This tiny ritual shifts the energy of the room. People feel seen, not just as employees, but as human beings.

Or consider a company that holds quarterly check-ins. But instead of diving straight into targets and metrics, they begin by asking, "What's been energizing you lately?" It is a simple question, but one that brings out stories of joy, curiosity, and purpose. Someone might talk about a project that allowed them to be creative. Another might speak of a mentor who supported them. These conversations may not directly affect revenue charts—but they build something far more valuable: connection and emotional clarity.

And the most beautiful thing? These rhythms do not need budgets or big plans. They just need intention. In a world where everything changes so fast, rhythms give us something steady to hold on to. They remind us that meaning does not come from doing more, but from doing the right things, again and again, with care.

These rhythms do not replace performance. They amplify it.

And then there's Relational Intelligence—a term we do not hear regularly. We speak of IQ, sometimes of EQ, but rarely of RQ. Yet, it is RQ that defines whether teams thrive or wither.

Relational intelligence is not a fancy term meant for boardrooms or psychological journals. It is, at its heart, the human ability to truly *notice*—to see beyond words, beyond performance, and into the emotional world of another person. It is the quiet skill of understanding how someone is really feeling, even when they're smiling and saying they're fine. It is about picking up on the subtle shifts—the silence that was not there yesterday, the hesitation in their voice, the camera that is turned off for the third time in a row.

It is the ability to sense when someone withdraws—not because they're being difficult or unproductive, but perhaps because they are overwhelmed, hurting, or simply exhausted. And then, to respond—not with a sharp question or a checklist, but with kindness. It is not asking, "What's wrong with you?" but gently saying, "I'm here if you need anything." Sometimes, no more than that is needed.

Relational intelligence does not require formal training. It begins with genuine care. I remember a manager who always carried a small diary. He did not use it to track numbers. He used it to jot down birthdays, a teammate's exam anxiety, or that someone's mother was in the hospital. These weren't data points. They were doorways to empathy. When someone felt off, he did not start with "Why are you late?" Instead, he said, "Is everything okay at home?"

Because at the end of the day, people do not remember what we said in meetings. They remember how we made them feel—especially when they were struggling.

It is also the wisdom to disagree without disrespect, to give feedback that uplifts instead of breaking, and to hold space for different working styles.

A friend who leads a team of nurses in a hospital once told me, "My team does not need more training. They need someone to sit with them after a long shift and say thank you." He was not being poetic. He was being practical.

In an age where we automate everything—from customer service to performance tracking—we must pause and remember a simple truth: humans are not algorithms. They are not lines of code to be optimized or predictable patterns to be managed. They feel deeply, carry invisible burdens, and sometimes stumble under pressures we cannot see. Yet, given the right environment, they also rise with remarkable strength, show compassion that machines cannot mimic, and build connections no system can replicate. To lead people well, we must honour this humanity—not just in strategy, but in our everyday interactions, choices, and values

So, how do we embed energy, empathy, and ethics?

1. **Energy**: Create rituals that restore, not just drain. A five-minute breathing break. A music hour. A wall of appreciation. These are not soft perks. These are human essentials.
2. **Empathy**: Build rhythms that check-in, not check-up. Make space for life conversations, not just work plans.
3. **Ethics**: Infuse relational intelligence in decision-making. Ask—what's the kindest way to handle this layoff? How can we be truthful and tender?

The organizations of the future will not be defined by skyscrapers with glass fronts, nap pods, or the latest AI-powered dashboards. They will not be remembered merely for how fast they processed data or how sleek their interfaces looked. Instead, they will be the ones who remember what makes us truly human—and designed everything around that remembering.

It is easy to be blinded by technology, to chase innovation for innovation's sake, and to lose sight of the people behind the progress. But amidst the noise of transformation, the companies that will thrive in the long run are those that ask softer, slower questions: Do our employees feel safe to speak up? Are people seen not just for what they produce but for who they are? Can someone pause, take a breath, and still feel valued in this system?

Because at the heart of every breakthrough—whether it is a product, a solution, or a service—there is a human story. A story of someone who dared, someone who cared, someone who took a risk not just with code but with courage.

Culture is not built in a day. But it is built every day.

And sometimes, it begins with a simple question: "How are you—really?"

The Calm Catalyst Truth #7:

"Sustainable culture is built on a code of energy, empathy, and ethics—the three circles of a workplace."

CHAPTER 8

INVISIBLE INFRASTRUCTURE – BEYOND STRATEGY AND STRUCTURE

8.1 The Importance of Unarticulated Values and Energetic Alignment

Let's start with a story.

In a quiet little office of a services firm in Bangalore, a new HR head once asked the founder, an elderly gentleman with peppered hair and a soft smile, "Sir, where are the company's core values documented? I could not find them in the induction folder."

The founder chuckled. "You won't find them in documents," he said. "You'll see them in how our receptionist speaks to a delivery boy. Or how we say no to clients when we cannot keep a promise. that is where our values live."

That sentence stayed with the HR head for a long time.

Unarticulated values—These are not the values you find printed in glossy brochures or etched proudly on glass doors in corporate lobbies. No, these are different. These are the values that live quietly in the hearts and actions of people. They are not spoken aloud at leadership summits or broadcast during annual town halls. Instead, they are deeply understood—almost instinctively felt—by those who walk the corridors and share tea in the pantry.

They are not taught in on boarding sessions or enforced by policies. Rather, they are absorbed through micro-moments—those small, seemingly ordinary instances that carry extraordinary meaning.

Like the way a senior manager quietly stays back to help a struggling intern, without ever mentioning it in their self-appraisal. Or when a team leader gently corrects an employee in private but praises them in public, never letting ego come in the way of growth. Or the way a janitor's birthday is remembered, just as the CEO's is, with the same warmth and regard.

At times, it is in the way a team offers a chair to the visiting delivery person, or how the receptionist smiles not just at clients, but at everyone who walks in. These are the subtle, yet powerful demonstrations of what a company truly values.

You see, real culture does not shout, it whispers. And those whispers are what create the atmosphere, the tone, the unspoken code of behaviour. Over time, these tiny gestures become part of the organization's nervous system—responding instinctively, operating smoothly, and holding everything together even during a storm.

The best part is nobody needs to remind anyone about these values. They are lived and passed on, like family traditions. They form the invisible fabric that binds people to each other—not by rules, but by respect. And that is a culture worth nurturing—not flashy, but deeply human.

These silent values become the energy signature of a workplace. They do not need approval flows. They just flow.

The Pulse Behind the Performance

A company may spend months crafting the perfect strategy. The slides will be polished, the goals ambitious, and the execution plan detailed down to the last decimal. On paper, it may look like a masterpiece. But if you walk through the corridors and feel a chill of fear, if the conversations are filled with cynicism, or if departments operate in silos—distrustful and distant—then that strategy, no matter how brilliant, will limp forward like a beautiful bird with a broken wing.

You see, work is not just what happens in meetings or on project trackers. Work is also what happens between the lines—during coffee breaks, in elevator rides, in hushed conversations after calls, and in the energy people carry when they show up each day. If that energy is heavy with suspicion, exhaustion, or emotional detachment, the best of plans will only get half-hearted participation.

Yes, people will follow instructions. They will tick boxes, meet deadlines, and attend meetings. But they will do so like machines—capable but empty. They may deliver outcomes, but those outcomes will lack soul. There will be no innovation, no emotional investment, no going the extra mile. And over time, that missing heart becomes visible—in customer feedback, in rising attrition, in the quiet withdrawal of once-enthusiastic employees.

Excellence does not thrive in a culture of compliance. It flourishes in an environment of care, trust, and shared purpose. When people feel safe, seen, and valued—not just for what they produce but for who they are—they begin to offer the best parts of themselves. Ideas spark. Collaboration deepens. Problems become shared puzzles rather than personal burdens.

So, before asking if the strategy is sound, ask if the energy is right. Are people merely following or are they belonging? Are they aligned not just by targets, but by trust?

Because where there is no heart, there is no excellence—only silent resignation in the face of well-written plans.

You see, energy is like the water under a lotus pond. You may only notice the flowers above, but without the clean water below, nothing blooms. Energetic alignment is this clean water.

It shows up when:

- Teams communicate openly, not just politely.
- People smile not to impress, but because they feel safe.
- Feedback is not a ritual, but a reflection.

The Cost of Energy Leaks

Have you ever stepped into an office and felt something heavy in the air? It is hard to explain, because nobody is shouting or complaining out loud. The meetings are on schedule, emails keep coming, and the usual corporate buzz carries on. Yet, before all this activity, there is a subtle but unmistakable tension. The energy feels off. You might notice people avoiding eye contact, conversations that lack warmth, or smiles that do not quite reach the eyes. It is as if the place is holding its breath, waiting for something to break.

This heaviness often comes from misalignment—when the values an organization proudly displays on its website or walls are not the ones lived every day. Values like "integrity," "collaboration," or "innovation" may sound inspiring in theory, but when people see behaviours that contradict those ideals, doubt creeps in. When leaders say one thing but do another, when kindness is preached but competitiveness rewarded, when openness is claimed but criticism punished, the gap between words and actions creates a silent rift.

People start to pretend. They learn which conversations are safe and which to avoid. They censor themselves, not because they do not have ideas or feelings, but because speaking up feels risky. Over time, this performance wears on everyone, draining authenticity and trust. Worse still, fear can become the default emotion—fear of making mistakes, fear of being judged, fear of losing status or job security. Fear is a heavy burden to carry to work every day.

When fear dominates, the workplace becomes a place of survival, not growth. People watch their backs instead of extending hands. Creativity withers under the pressure to conform. Engagement drops, and morale falters. This invisible atmosphere affects not just individuals, but teams, departments, and the entire organization's ability to move forward with confidence and heart.

These energy leaks show up in:

- Passive meetings with little ownership
- Teams that avoid difficult conversations
- High attrition, despite attractive salaries

Companies often react by redesigning workflows or introducing new tech. But what they need is **alignment repair**—a conscious effort to reconnect people to purpose, respect, and mutual belief.

Bringing Energetic Alignment to Life

Some leaders create energy alignment not through grand speeches or sweeping declarations, but through small, steady acts of consistency. It is not the big, flashy moments that shape culture; it is the everyday actions that quietly ripple through the organization and build trust over time. For example, a leader who always listens fully when someone is speaking—without glancing at their phone or checking emails—sends a powerful message. That simple act shows respect, presence, and genuine care. It says, "You matter. Your words matter."

Similarly, acknowledging invisible contributions is another way energy alignment happens. These are the things that often go unnoticed but make a huge difference in how people feel at work. Think of the team member who quietly checks every lunch order for allergies, ensuring no one is excluded or put at risk. Or the IT person who notices the printer is jammed and fixes it without being asked, so the whole team can keep working smoothly. These small gestures may seem minor, but they create a feeling of being cared for and seen.

An inspiring example comes from a Bengaluru-based firm that introduced an innovative idea called a "culture audit." But this was not a typical HR-driven exercise. Instead, the process was led by peers, encouraging everyone in the company to notice and celebrate the everyday acts that bring the company's values to life. Every month, employees could nominate colleagues who embodied the spirit of the firm—not by how well they hit their KPIs or targets, but by the genuine care they showed in their work and interactions.

One month, a designer was nominated because she stayed late into the night to help a struggling teammate meet a tight deadline. Another time, a cleaner in the office was recognized for leaving little thank-you notes in the pantry, brightening the day for anyone who found them. These nominations were not about grand gestures but about recognizing the quiet dedication and kindness that make a workplace feel human.

This "culture audit" became a powerful way to surface and celebrate the invisible contributions that otherwise might go unnoticed. It encouraged everyone to pay attention to what really matters: how we treat each other day to day. More importantly, it showed that leadership is not only about the people at the top. Leadership happens in every role, every corner, whenever someone chooses care and consistency over convenience.

In this way, energy alignment is less about slogans and more about the little things—the small acts that signal respect, empathy, and connection.

Each story became a mirror of values—not declared but discovered.

What Can We Learn?

1. Values are not declared; they are demonstrated.
2. Alignment begins with leaders who live the invisible values.
3. When energy flows right, performance follows naturally.

As elders often say, "Do not ask a child to be honest. Be honest yourself." The same goes for culture.

Let organizations stop screaming about values and start living them silently.

8.2 Systemic Thinking – Seeing What Holds the System Together

I once met a school principal who shared a simple but interesting insight with me. She said, "I do not just see the students. I see the environment around them—the teacher's mood, the support staff's attitude, the walls of the classroom. All of it teaches the child." At first, it sounded like a small observation, but the more I thought about it, the more I realized how deeply true it is—not only in schools but in every organization and community.

We often focus so much on individuals—the star performer, the struggling student, and the manager who delivers results — that we forget about the larger environment that shapes them. The principal reminded me that children do not learn in isolation. They absorb everything—the smiles or sighs of their teachers, the respect or indifference shown by the janitor, even the cleanliness or clutter of the classroom walls. These elements speak a silent language, a constant background hum that shapes how children feel, how they behave, and how they grow.

If in a classroom where a teacher walks in tired and frustrated. Even if she tries to hide it, the children feel the tension. They become restless or withdrawn. Now again, the same room, but the teacher enters with warmth, a gentle smile, and patience. The energy shifts. The children feel safe and ready to learn. It is not just about what is taught in lessons; it is about the emotional climate that carries those lessons.

The principal also spoke about the support staff—the custodians, the office helpers, the security personnel. Many adults may think their work is separate from the children's learning, but every interaction sends a message. A custodian who greets children warmly at the door makes them feel welcome and valued. A security guard who patiently listens to a student's worries becomes a quiet pillar of safety. These small acts of kindness create a ripple effect that can transform the entire school environment.

She even pointed out the physical environment—the walls, the colours, the decorations, the cleanliness. A classroom filled with bright colours, inspiring quotes, and children's artwork feels alive and encouraging. On the other hand, dull, neglected spaces can sap energy and enthusiasm. The physical surroundings, often overlooked, are an unspoken teacher.

This insight made me think about workplaces as well. Just like a school, a workplace is not just about the people on paper or the tasks they perform. It is about the entire environment—the tone set by leaders, the respect shown by colleagues, the small rituals that make people feel connected, and the physical space itself. When these elements align positively, they create a fertile ground where people can thrive.

The principal's perspective invites us to look beyond the obvious. It asks us to consider what messages our environments are sending. Are they nurturing or neglectful? Are they filled with care or burdened by indifference? The answers matter deeply because we do not exist in isolation. We are shaped by the spaces and people around us.

In the end, leadership is not just about managing tasks or setting goals. It is about cultivating an environment where everyone—whether a child in a classroom or an employee in an office—feels seen, supported, and inspired to grow. This holistic view reminds us that every detail counts, and every person, no matter their role, contributes to the invisible classroom we all live and learn.

That is what **systemic thinking** is.

It is seeing the whole—not just the parts.

Beyond the Org Chart

In most companies, when we think about performance, we tend to look at it through the lens of individuals or departments. We say, "Sales did well this quarter," or "Marketing lagged behind their targets." It is easy to focus on these parts because they are measurable and visible. But a company is never just a collection of isolated parts. It is a living system—a complex web of relationships, connections, and interactions that hold it all together. To truly understand how a company performs, we need to look beyond individual numbers and examine the entire network of relationships that sustain it.

Think of a spider's web. At first glance, it might seem delicate, but it is incredibly strong. If you touch one corner of the web, the vibration travels through every strand, no matter how far. That is how culture in an organization works—it is not confined to one person or one team. The energy, attitudes, and behaviours of one part affect the entire system. When one part suffers, the whole network feels it.

For example, consider a team leader who is toxic—someone who undermines their team, creates tension, or spreads negativity. The immediate effect is on the team's morale. But the impact does not stop there. That tension seeps outward, affecting how the team interacts with other departments. The salespeople might hesitate to collaborate, customer service may face challenges when the team fails to deliver on promises, and innovation slows down because people are too wary or stressed to take risks.

It does not end with internal teams. Even external partners and vendors can sense this disruption. When a supplier notices friction or poor communication from one department, they might become hesitant or cautious in their dealings. Over time, this can erode trust and harm long-term relationships that are key for business success.

Conversely, when leaders cultivate positivity, trust, and collaboration, the web strengthens. The ripples are felt everywhere—increased creativity, better teamwork, higher customer satisfaction, and even improved vendor relations. It creates a virtuous cycle where energy flows freely, and everyone feels connected to a common purpose.

This understanding calls for a shift in how we approach organizational health. Instead of evaluating isolated pockets of performance, we must recognize the interconnectedness of every role, every action, and every decision. A great product team means little if the sales team feels unsupported. High individual performance is less valuable if collaboration breaks down.

In the end, success is not about a single star shining brightest, but about how the constellation holds together. The health of the entire web, the invisible threads of culture and connection, determines whether a company thrives or merely survives.

Systemic leaders ask different questions:

- Not: "Who made the mistake?"
- But: "What in the system made the mistake easy to happen?"

This shift from blame to pattern recognition is the true art of leadership.

8.3 The Unseen Glue

At an IT company in Bangalore, a shipment of critical hardware went missing. It was not a small issue; the missing equipment delayed important projects and put customer commitments at risk. Naturally, the initial reaction was to find who was responsible. Was it the logistics team? The warehouse staff? The procurement department? But as the investigation unfolded, something unexpected occurred—no single person could be blamed.

Instead, what became clear was a pattern of confusion and unclear handoffs between departments. The flow of responsibility was tangled. Job titles overlapped, making it difficult to know who was accountable for each step. When one team completed their part, it was unclear exactly where their work ended and the next team's responsibility began. This gray area was a breeding ground for mistakes, misunderstandings, and, ultimately, the missing shipment.

In many organizations, this situation would have led to blame games, finger-pointing, or even firing someone to set an example. But the CEO of this company took a different path. She called all the involved teams together and said, "Let's look at the system, not just the symptom." Instead of hunting for a scapegoat, she encouraged everyone to see how the entire process was connected and how the system itself was leaking energy and efficiency.

They sat down to map out the entire flow of the hardware shipment process, step by step. They identified where the handoffs happened, where information was lost or delayed, and where responsibilities were unclear. This exercise revealed that the problem was not individual negligence but a structural gap—a system that was not designed to support smooth collaboration.

Together, the teams redesigned the workflow. They clarified interfaces—who does what, when, and how. They drew clear boundaries and defined points of accountability. More importantly, they did not stop at roles and processes; they agreed on new cross-functional rituals to keep communication open.

The change was remarkable. The same people who had struggled before were now performing much better. Not because they were working harder or longer hours, but because the system had stopped leaking energy. They no longer wasted time chasing answers or fixing avoidable errors. The clear flow and shared rituals created a sense of mutual trust and ownership.

What can we learn from this story?

First, it reminds us that organizations are systems, not just a collection of individuals. When problems arise, the solution often lies in examining how the parts fit together, rather than blaming one person. Accountability in a system is shared, and clarity of roles and handoffs is key.

Second, it shows the power of leadership that moves beyond blame. The CEO's choice to bring people together and focus on systemic fixes rather than punishment created a safe space for collaboration and continuous improvement.

Third, it highlights those improving systems means more than fixing processes. It requires building relationships, improving communication rituals, and nurturing a culture where teams feel connected and aligned.

This story is a gentle nudge to leaders and organizations: Instead of rushing to point fingers when things go wrong, pause and ask, "What is the system telling us?" Because sometimes, the problem is not a person but the structure that holds them.

And the best solutions come when we listen carefully, collaborate deeply, and design thoughtfully.

This is the unseen glue—shared understanding and role clarity.

The Calm Catalyst Truth #8:

"It is not the noise of strategy, but the silence of systems that holds an organization together."

CHAPTER 9

THE INNER BOARDROOM: LEADERSHIP FROM THE INSIDE OUT

9.1 The Evolving Role of Self-Awareness, Spirituality, and Introspection

Leadership is often seen as something that happens, outwardly guiding teams, making strategic decisions, motivating others, and steering organizations toward goals. When we think of leadership, we tend to picture someone standing at the forefront, giving directions, setting targets, or inspiring crowds. The spotlight is usually on actions that influence external results: meeting sales goals, launching new products, or transforming company culture. Yet, this external view, while important, misses a fact. What if the deepest and lasting leadership begins within? What if the secret to truly effective leadership lies not just in what we do externally but in the invisible inner world that shapes our every decision and interaction?

This hidden space—the "inner boardroom"—is the private space inside each leader where thoughts, emotions, values, and beliefs quietly reside. It is where self-awareness grows, where clarity and purpose take root, and where resilience is built in the face of uncertainty. While the external boardroom discusses market strategies, financials, and project plans, the inner boardroom wrestles with questions about integrity, intention, and emotional balance. It is here that leaders decide how to respond to challenges, how to handle stress, and how to stay connected to their deeper purpose.

Without a strong inner boardroom, even the most impressive external leadership can falter. A leader who is unaware of their own fears, biases, or emotional triggers may unintentionally create discord or lose sight of what truly matters. Conversely, leaders who cultivate their inner boardroom—by reflecting on their values, understanding their emotions, and nurturing self-awareness—bring a grounded presence that inspires trust and loyalty.

The inner boardroom shapes a leader's ability to navigate complexity. where uncertainty and rapid change are the norms, external strategies alone are insufficient. Leaders must adapt not only their plans but their mindset. This requires a calm, clear, and focused inner space—a place where impulsive reactions are replaced by thoughtful responses, where empathy balances decisiveness, and where vision is infused with humility.

In essence, leadership from the inside out is a powerful shift. It invites us to recognize that leadership effectiveness is not just measured by what we achieve externally but by how well we manage and nurture the inner space that guides our actions. The real power lies in cultivating this invisible space—the inner boardroom—because it is from here that authentic, resilient, and transformative leadership blooms

But what do these terms really mean? And how do they connect to the way we lead?

Questioning the Fundamentals:

- What does it mean to be self-aware as a leader?

Is self-awareness just knowing your strengths and weaknesses? Or is it a deeper understanding of your motives, fears, and habitual patterns? Can a leader lead others effectively without truly knowing themselves?

- How does spirituality fit into leadership?

Is spirituality only about religion, or is it a universal human experience of connection, purpose, and meaning? Can a spiritual outlook help leaders navigate ethical dilemmas, build compassion, and create purpose-driven organizations?

- Why is introspection so often neglected in leadership development?

Are we so focused on external achievements that we ignore inner reflection? What are we missing when we do?

Exploring Self-Awareness:

True self-awareness is often misunderstood as a quick fix or a one-time exercise. Many people assume it can be captured by a simple personality test, a 360-degree feedback survey, or a brief reflection session. While these tools can offer helpful insights, they merely scratch the surface. True self-awareness goes much deeper—it is a continuous, unfolding journey that requires courage, honesty, and persistence. It is a lifelong process of looking inward with an open heart and a clear mind, seeking to understand not only the parts of ourselves we are proud of but also the aspects we might rather avoid or deny.

At its core, true self-awareness involves recognizing your emotional triggers—the moments when certain situations, words, or behaviours provoke strong reactions within you. These triggers often point to unresolved fears, insecurities, or past wounds. For example, a leader might find themselves unusually irritated during meetings when a colleague challenges their ideas. This irritation is rarely about the challenge itself; more often, it is about an underlying fear of being seen as incompetent or losing control. By becoming aware of these emotional triggers, leaders gain the power to pause, reflect, and respond thoughtfully rather than react impulsively.

Understanding your biases is another critical dimension of self-awareness. Every individual carries unconscious beliefs shaped by their upbringing, culture, and experiences. These biases influence how we perceive others, make decisions, and interact with the world—often without our conscious knowledge. For example, a manager might unconsciously favour employees who share their background or communication style, inadvertently limiting diversity and inclusion. Developing true self-awareness means shining a light on these blind spots, questioning assumptions, and actively seeking perspectives that challenge our preconceived notions.

Perhaps the most challenging aspect of self-awareness is facing your shadows—the parts of yourself that are uncomfortable, unwanted, or socially unacceptable. These might include tendencies toward impatience, insecurity, envy, or fear of failure. Often, these shadows are hidden under the layers of defence mechanisms, denial, or self-justification. Yet, it is precisely by acknowledging and embracing these darker aspects that leaders become whole and authentic.

The journey of self-awareness is rarely comfortable. It can evoke feelings of doubt, discomfort, and even shame. But it is this discomfort that fuels growth. Like a muscle that strengthens through resistance, self-awareness expands through honest self-examination and reflection. Practices such as journaling, meditation, mindful listening, and honest conversations with trusted mentors or coaches can support this ongoing process.

Ultimately, true self-awareness transforms leadership from a position of authority into a practice of presence. Leaders who cultivate this deep inner understanding are better equipped to navigate complexity, build trust, and inspire others. They lead with empathy because they have learned to listen to their own inner voices. They make decisions with clarity because they understand their motivations and limitations.

World that celebrates quick results and surface-level achievements, true self-awareness invites leaders to slow down, turn inward, and embrace the ongoing journey of becoming. It is a thoughtful path that not only shapes better leaders but also creates more compassionate, authentic, and thriving organizations

The Power of Spirituality in Leadership:

In the busy corridors of the corporate world—where quarterly results dominate meetings, competition drives decision-making, and technological innovations disrupt markets—there is an often-overlooked dimension that can deeply reshape leadership and organizational culture: spirituality. Not the narrowly defined, religious sense of spirituality, but its broadest, most inclusive understanding. Spirituality invites leaders to connect with something far greater than themselves—a sense of purpose, a commitment to values that transcend profit, and a deep recognition of the interconnectedness that binds individuals, organizations, and society.

At first glance, this might seem at odds with the relentless pace and pragmatism of business. After all, corporations measure success through metrics—revenue growth, market share, efficiency ratios—not through spiritual awakenings. Yet, precisely because of constant pressures, rapid change, and deep societal challenges, spirituality has become not a luxury but a necessity in leadership.

From Transactional to Transformational Leadership

Traditional leadership models often treat the role as transactional: leaders set goals, assign tasks, monitor performance, and reward or correct as defined. It is a mechanistic, cause-and-effect approach that works well when the environment is stable, predictable, and linear. But the corporate world today is anything but stable or predictable. Hybrid work, AI-driven automation, global uncertainties, and shifting employee expectations demand a different kind of leadership—one that is not just about managing outcomes but about inspiring and transforming people.

Spirituality offers this transformation. When leaders connect their work to a higher purpose—a calling beyond profit margins or personal ambition—they become transformational leaders. They inspire commitment not through fear or incentive, but through shared values and meaning. This shift from a transactional to a transformational mindset is essential because people are not mere resources; they are human beings who seek connection, significance, and contribution.

Ethics and Compassion as Corporate Pillars

Spirituality naturally brings ethics and compassion to the forefront of leadership. In a world where scandals and corporate misbehaviour make headlines, ethical lapses often stem from short-term thinking and disconnection from deeper values. Leaders grounded in spirituality recognize that their actions ripple beyond balance sheets—to employees, communities, customers, and even the environment.

This awareness builds culture, where ethical behaviour is not imposed as compliance but embraced as a shared responsibility. Compassion flows naturally, enabling leaders to approach challenges with empathy and understanding. This is not about being soft or naive—it is about cultivating emotional intelligence and moral courage, which are essential for sustainable success in complex environments.

A Practical Call to Leaders

Integrating spirituality into leadership is not about abandoning the rigors of business. It is about enriching leadership with qualities that honour the full humanity of people and the interconnected nature of organizations and society. It invites leaders to ask reflective questions: Why do I lead? What legacy do I want to leave? How do my actions serve the greater good?

Organizations can support this journey by creating spaces for reflection, encouraging authentic conversations about values, and modelling leadership behaviours that embody spiritual principles. Training programs might include emotional intelligence, mindfulness, and ethical decision-making, and purpose-driven leadership.

The Role of Introspection:

Introspection is the gentle act of turning inward, of peering quietly into one's own mind and heart to understand what lies under the surface. It is not about overthinking or obsessing over every decision. Rather, it is a practice of honest self-inquiry—of examining one's thoughts, emotions, motivations, and reactions without judgment or haste. In a world that constantly demands action and urgency, introspection offers a rare and needed pause. It is the still breath between two sentences, the silence that speaks louder than noise.

For leaders, introspection is a necessity. Every day, leaders face decisions that impact not only bottom lines but also people's lives and careers. The pressure to perform, to meet deadlines, to respond instantly, can lead to reactive behaviours and rushed judgments. Without a practice of regular introspection, it becomes easy to lose sight of one's values, to get swept away by external expectations, or to confuse motion with meaning.

Introspection allows leaders to pause and ask the questions that matter: Why am I feeling resistance to this change? Is my decision aligned with our core purpose? Am I reacting from fear, ego, or clarity? These moments of reflection build the muscle of acumen—the ability to separate noise from signal, impulse from insight.

More importantly, introspection builds empathy. A leader who understands their own struggles, triggers, and emotional patterns is better equipped to understand those of others. They listen more deeply. They lead not just with goals, but with grace. Employees sense this difference. It shows in how these leaders respond to failure, handle conflict, and celebrate small, meaningful wins. It creates cultures of psychological safety—where people feel seen, heard, and respected.

Corporate organizations today would do well to normalize and encourage introspection. This could be through reflective leadership retreats, end-of-week journaling prompts, or simply creating a culture where pausing is not seen as a weakness but as wisdom. In a team where leaders ask not just "What did we achieve?" but also "What did we learn about ourselves this week?"

Introspection is not just an inner dialogue—it is a leadership tool. It transforms reactivity into reflection, confusion into clarity, and ambition into purpose. In the inner boardroom of the mind, introspection is the quiet chair where the truest decisions are made. And for leaders steering the complexity, that quiet chair may just be the most powerful seat they'll ever hold.

Showing the Way Forward:

- Encourage leaders to build daily habits of self-reflection, such as journaling or mindful pauses.
- Promote leadership programs that integrate emotional intelligence, mindfulness, and ethical inquiry.
- Create organizational cultures that value inner work as much as outer performance.

Leadership today disguises itself in metrics, milestones, and management tools. But under the surface, the most fundamental decisions are shaped not by external frameworks but by inner stability. The real battles of leadership—doubt, fear, values, identity—are quiet and internal.

In Mahabharat, long before the first arrow on the battlefield of Kurukshetra, a different war stormed within Arjuna—a war not of swords, but of spirit. Challenged with the prospect of fighting his own kin, Arjuna crumbled, not from fear of death, but from the weight of duty, emotion, and inner conflict. It was then that Krishna did not hand him a battle plan or a motivational speech—he handed him a mirror. The *Bhagavad Gita*, often mistaken as a scripture, is in truth a dialogue of leadership—a thoughtful separating of self-doubt, ego, detachment, and higher purpose. In that sacred moment, the battlefield became an inner boardroom. Arjuna was not a warrior being coached; he was a leader learning to lead from the inside out. Like Arjuna, modern leaders often stand at crossroads covered in silence—unsure, conflicted, and isolated. The answers are rarely outside. True clarity, like Krishna's guidance, emerges only when we turn inward, past the noise, into the still chamber of the self. That is where the real leadership begins—not with command, but with consciousness.

This inner boardroom is not theoretical. It exists in every pause before a difficult decision, in the discomfort of self-reflection, and in the moments when silence speaks louder than direction. The practices we explore ahead—stillness, self-inquiry, and presence—are not luxuries but tools for navigating this invisible chamber. For those willing to listen, the voice of clarity is already within.

9.2 Practices for Cultivating Inner Stability and Clarity in Leaders

If the inner boardroom is where leadership begins, how do leaders cultivate stability and clarity in this space? How do they navigate the inner storms of doubt, fear, and distraction that all humans face?

Leadership practices that nurture inner calm are not luxuries—they are essentials. They help leaders respond instead of reacting, listen deeply instead of dominating, and make decisions rooted in wisdom rather than impulse.

Questioning the Fundamentals:

- What happens when leaders lack inner stability?

Does anxiety ripple through the team? Do decisions become erratic? What costs do we pay when leaders are ruled by inner turmoil?

- Is clarity something that can be taught, or is it only discovered?

Can external practices cultivate clarity, or is it purely an inner awakening?

- How do we balance ambition and humility on this journey?

Can leaders remain driven and yet grounded, confident and yet curious?

Essential Practices for Inner Stability:

1. Mindfulness and Meditation:
   The simplest and most accessible practice to anchor the mind. It is not about escaping problems but meeting them with calm attention. Regular mindfulness helps leaders notice their thoughts and emotions without being overwhelmed.
2. Journaling:
   Writing down thoughts, feelings, and reflections can illuminate unconscious patterns and bring clarity. It acts as a conversation with oneself, a mirror for the soul.
3. Seeking Solitude:
   In a world obsessed with constant connectivity, solitude is revolutionary. It offers space for deep listening and reconnecting with core values.
4. Breathwork and Physical Awareness:
   Our body holds our stress and emotions. Practices that connect breath and body awareness help regulate emotions and ground the mind.
5. Ethical Reflection:

Regularly questioning the alignment of actions with values builds integrity and trustworthiness.

Cultivating Clarity in Decision-Making:

Clarity is often mistaken for certainty. Many believe that if you read enough reports, analyse enough data, and attend enough strategy meetings, clarity will automatically develop. But that is not always true. In fact, the more information we have, the harder it sometimes becomes to see clearly. Like a windshield blurred by too many raindrops, too much input without reflection only creates fog. Real clarity, the kind that enables wise and courageous decisions, is not just about intellect. It is born out of integration—when the mind and heart align.

In leadership, clarity cannot be a one-dimensional trait. A decision that looks good on paper may not always feel right in the gut. A policy driven purely by metrics may harm team morale in unseen ways. That is why great leaders cultivate the ability to listen to both their analytical mind and their intuitive wisdom. They balance logic with empathy, numbers with narratives, and outcomes with ethics.

Let's take an example. A leader is faced with a decision to close down an underperforming branch. The spreadsheets show declining revenues. The projections point to losses. The logical choice seems clear. But this leader pauses. She visits the branch. Talks to the staff. Learns that the drop in performance was due to a family tragedy faced by the branch manager. She also notices a deep sense of ownership among the team and a strong bond with the local community. She does not reverse her decision out of sentimentality. Instead, she sees the bigger picture. She initiates support to stabilize the team and gives the branch a six-month turnaround window. In the end, the branch recovers, and more importantly, the team grows stronger in loyalty and performance.

What changed the outcome was not a different set of facts—it was clarity rooted in both data and compassion. Clarity of this nature requires more than intelligence. It requires presence. Leaders who are fully present—who are not distracted by ego, fear, or external noise—develop a sharper lens. They do not rush into decisions to feel powerful. They pause to understand. They consult, they reflect, they ask deeper questions. And in those moments of pause, wisdom develops.

One powerful way to cultivate clarity is through reflective decision-making exercises. This does not require hours of meditation. It could be a simple five-minute pause before making a major decision. During this pause, a leader can ask:

- "Am I reacting or responding?"
- "Is this aligned with our values?"
- "What would be the impact of this decision one year from now?"
- "Who might be affected who is not in the room today?"

These questions create space between provocation and response. That space is where clarity is born.

Another important pathway to clarity is seeking diverse perspectives. No leader, even with experience, can see the full picture alone. Every person carries blind spots—areas they do not see due to their background, personality, or position. Wise leaders actively invite differing viewpoints. They listen to the youngest intern, the quietest colleague, the most critical voice. Not to agree with all, but to widen their own field of vision. When clarity is crowd-sourced, it becomes resilient. It stands the test of challenge because it is not rooted in a single point of view.

Clarity is also about alignment. Alignment between what is said and what is done. Between personal values and organizational actions. A leader who says "people matter" but ignores employee feedback sends mixed signals. That confusion spreads, creating mistrust.

Clarity also thrives when leaders evaluate decisions with a long-term lens. Many organizations reward short-term wins—quarterly profits, rapid turnarounds. But clarity invites leaders to ask, "Will this benefit the system over time?" Sometimes the right decision in the short run may not be the wisest one in the long run. Choosing to invest in employee well-being may cost more today, but create loyalty, innovation, and stability tomorrow.

In the final analysis, clarity in leadership is not just about making the right decision—it is about *becoming* the kind of person from whom right decisions naturally evolve. A person who listens deeply, thinks holistically, and acts from a place of internal steadiness. When leaders operate from such clarity, they do not just reduce errors—they elevate the entire energy of the organization. People feel safe. Teams move with direction. Cultures become more humane.

Inner leadership is not a soft skill—it is a *core capacity*. It is the silent force behind clear strategy, strong execution, and meaningful relationships. Leaders who invest in their own stability and clarity do not just perform—they transform. They leave legacies not because of how fast they led, but because of how deeply they touched the lives around them.

And in a world that is constantly looking for the next big innovation, perhaps the biggest innovation in leadership is simply this: returning to oneself.

The Calm Catalyst Truth #9:

"The strongest leaders are not those who speak the loudest, but those who listen within the deepest."

PART IV

THE POWER OF QUIET INFLUENCE

CHAPTER 10

THE INVISIBLE LEADERSHIP -THE QUIET FORCE BEHIND TRANSFORMATIONAL IMPACT

The Night the Engines Went Silent: How Calmness Saved 263 Lives at 37,000 Feet

On the night of June 24, 1982, British Airways Flight 9, a Boeing 747 named *City of Edinburgh*, cruised above the Indian Ocean on what should have been just another leg of its journey from London to Auckland. The cabin lights were dim. Passengers sipped tea or dozed. The flight crew settled into the rhythm of a long-haul night flight.

Then, without warning, the sky changed.

Outside, darkness turned metallic. The stars disappeared, replaced by a shining haze. Flight Officer Roger Greaves noticed something strange—a blue glow around the engines. It looked like static electricity.

But beautiful things at 37,000 feet can turn deadly in seconds.

Inside the cockpit, all four Rolls-Royce engines began to surge. Then they failed. One by one. In under two minutes, the 747 became a 300-ton glider.

The cockpit fell into weird silence. No engine hum. Just alarms. Lights flashed. Altitude dropped. They were still over open water, nowhere near an airport. No engine meant no power. No power meant no air conditioning, no pressurization, and no way to hold altitude for long.

Panic should have taken over.

But it didn't.

Because Captain Eric Moody, in that exact moment, chose a tone that would define everything that came next.

He calmly picked up the intercom and said, with understated British clarity:

"Ladies and gentlemen, this is your captain speaking. We have a small problem. All four engines have stopped. We are doing our utmost to get them going. I trust you are not in too much distress."

No dramatics. No screaming. Just presence.

The Anatomy of Calm

Eric Moody was not minimizing the danger. He understood the gravity. But he also understood this: panic amplifies problems. Calm reduces them.

It is a principle you see in everything from crisis negotiations to top sports teams: The environment takes cues from the leader's nervous system.

The flight crew—Moody, Senior First Officer Roger Greaves, and Flight Engineer Barry Townley-Freeman—had trained for emergencies. But this was not a scenario in the manual. Volcanic ash was not even part of their risk awareness. They did not know what they had flown into. But they knew one thing: they had to glide. And fast.

From their altitude, they had roughly 20 minutes before hitting the water.

Every minute counted.

The crew ran checklists. They tried engine restart sequences. Nothing worked. The cockpit windows turned opaque with ash abrasion. Cabin oxygen masks deployed. Some passengers wept. Others sat still, too stunned to speak. But something strange was happening—the calm voice of the captain had landed like an anchor.

People weren't screaming.

They were listening.

They were trusting.

This was not luck. It was leadership by design.

Mid-Crisis Turning Point: One Engine Sparks Back

As the aircraft descended through 26,000 feet, something extraordinary happened. Engine 4 roared back to life. Then another. And another.

The volcanic ash—composed of microscopic glass particles—had choked the engines at high altitude. But as the aircraft dropped into denser, cooler air, the engines cooled enough to relight.

It was not over. But it was no longer a free fall.

Still, visibility was near zero. Ash had sandblasted the windshield. The crew could not see the runway. And they had to land—a night landing in Jakarta, on limited power, with a partially functioning aircraft.

Calm did not mean lack of urgency. It meant control of emotion under urgency.

As they approached the runway, Captain Moody and his crew executed a near-blind landing, guided largely by ground control and gut feel. The 747 touched down safely.

263 lives. Saved by four re-lit engines—and the self-control of a crew who never gave their fear the microphone.

Behavioural Insights: What the Flight Taught Us

1. Calm is Contagious

Had Captain Moody panicked, the flight attendants would have panicked. The passengers would have followed. At 37,000 feet, collective panic is not just frightening—it's fatal.

Calm behaviour, especially from leaders, creates emotional control. It regulates the psychological climate of a team. This applies as much in boardrooms as in cockpits.

2. Language Shapes Experience

"Small problem" may seem like a comical understatement. But Moody's wording was intentional. Language frames emotion.

When we label situations as "disasters" or "impossible," we invite helplessness. When we say "challenge," "signal," or "glitch," we create psychological room for response.

You do not lie. You lead with clarity minus the chaos.

3. Training Buys Time, Calm Buys Choices

The flight crew did not invent new skills mid-air. They reverted to well-practiced checklists, layered with instinct. But training alone does not explain their performance.

What really mattered? Their capacity to stay present. To not rush. To not scream. The mind, under stress, wants to leap to conclusions.

4. Quiet Doesn't Mean Inaction

In moments of silence—engines off, glider-mode descending—there was intense activity inside that cockpit. But it did not look panicky.

Calm is not passive. It is deliberate energy applied with control.

5. Leadership Is Most Visible When Results Are Not

No passenger could see inside the cockpit. But they could feel the effect of the crew's choices.

The best leadership is often invisible—but felt. In tone, in presence, in the trust it promotes.

What Captain Moody and his crew demonstrated that night was not dramatic heroism. It was something quieter and more stable—**invisible leadership born from calm awareness.** They did not command the cabin with volume. They shaped its emotional climate through **presence, self-control, and precise checks**. When all four engines failed, what truly held the aircraft aloft was not just aerodynamics—it was the weightless power of **emotional steadiness**.

10.1 The Paradox of Leadership

When we think of leadership, what image usually comes to mind? A powerful figure standing on a stage, commanding attention with bold speeches. A decisive individual making tough calls in the boardroom, the centre of every major meeting. Or perhaps a charismatic presence whose very name invokes awe and respect throughout the company. Leadership, we often assume, is a role defined by visibility — by being seen and heard, by standing tall in the spotlight.

But what if this familiar image only tells half the story? What if the most powerful leaders in our organizations are not the loudest voices or the most visible figures? What if they are the ones we barely notice — the people who do not seek applause, do not crave recognition, and never demand the spotlight? These are the Invisible Leaders — the silent architects of corporate success.

Invisible leadership is a paradox. It challenges our fundamental assumptions about what it means to lead. It reminds us that leadership is not always about control, authority, or dominance. Instead, it is about presence, consistency, humility, and influence that runs deep and wide — often in ways too subtle to measure by traditional means.

The Story of Ravi: A Leader You Might Not Notice

Take Ravi, for example, a mid-level manager at a large multinational company. Ravi's name rarely comes up in leadership meetings. He does not have a flashy title, nor does he command an entourage of assistants. You won't find him giving keynote speeches or featured on the company's website. But ask around, and you'll find many who consider Ravi the heartbeat of his division.

Why? Because Ravi leads in ways that do not make headlines but deeply impact people's everyday work lives.

One afternoon, the team faced a major challenge: a critical project was behind schedule, tensions were high, and the usual senior leaders were too busy with other priorities to step in. Instead of escalating the issue, Ravi quietly stayed late, meeting one-on-one with team members to understand their roadblocks. He listened patiently as frustration poured out, never interrupting or judging. Instead, he offered thoughtful suggestions and, more importantly, promised to advocate for them in the next management meeting.

The next day, Ravi arranged for other resources and adjusted deadlines to reduce pressure. He sent brief notes of encouragement to his team, acknowledging the hard work they were putting in — even if those notes never made it into the official company newsletter.

To an outsider, Ravi's actions seemed small and almost invisible. But the effect was deep. The team felt seen and supported. Morale improved, productivity increased, and the project eventually met its goals.

Ravi never sought recognition for these efforts. He was not managing up for praise or positioning himself for a promotion. His leadership was not about status or spotlight; it was about quietly enabling others to succeed.

What Makes Invisible Leadership So Powerful?

Ravi's story highlights a truth about leadership that often gets lost: the deepest influence is seldom loud or overt. Invisible leaders wield power not by issuing commands but by embodying qualities that inspire trust, safety, and growth.

1. Humility Over Pride

Invisible leaders understand a fundamental truth that many overlook: leadership is not about being the hero or seeking the spotlight. Unlike those who crave recognition or need constant validation, these leaders operate without ego. They do not feel the urge to prove themselves or dominate conversations to assert their worth. Instead, their focus shifts from personal acclaim to something far more meaningful — the success and growth of the entire team. They recognize that every individual, regardless of role or rank, brings unique strengths and perspectives that contribute to collective achievement.

This deep humility sets the tone for the entire organization. When a leader prioritizes the team's goals over personal glory, it sends a powerful message: each person's contribution matters and is respected. Such an environment encourages trust and openness. People feel safe to share ideas, take risks, and innovate because they know they won't be overshadowed or dismissed. They feel empowered rather than intimidated, motivated rather than expendable.

In this culture, the energy flows freely. Collaboration thrives, and the organization moves forward as a cohesive, inspired unit. Invisible leadership, rooted in humility, creates fertile ground for sustainable success — where everyone wins, together.

2. Consistency Over Flashiness

Consistency is the quiet heartbeat of trust. Invisible leaders understand this deeply, and they show up every single day with unwavering dedication and integrity. Unlike flashy displays or grand announcements, their leadership is marked by the small, reliable actions they repeat time and again. These seemingly simple behaviours—if it is following over on promises, being punctual, offering a steady presence during crises, or listening attentively—build a reservoir of trust that no dramatic gesture alone can match.

When a leader is consistent, people feel safe. They know what to expect, and that certainty creates a stable environment where individuals can focus on their work without the distraction of unpredictability or doubt. This kind of trust acts as a protective shield during difficult times—when markets falter, deadlines loom, or conflict arises. Employees and teams gain confidence because they trust their leader will remain steady and reliable, no matter the storm.

Consistency also shapes organizational culture. When leaders embody integrity and dedication day after day, those values ripple through the team. People start mirroring the same commitment, creating a chain reaction of accountability and dependability. This collective reliability becomes a cornerstone for long-term success.

In essence, consistency is not flashy, but it is deeply powerful. It forms the invisible infrastructure upon which trust is built, empowering organizations to navigate uncertainty with resilience and confidence. Invisible leaders know this truth and live by it—quietly, persistently, and effectively.

3. Service Over Authority

Invisible leaders lead by serving. Their leadership style turns traditional notions of authority upside down. Instead of demanding obedience or expecting blind compliance, these leaders put the needs of their people first. They understand that true leadership is not about commanding from the top but about empowering those around them. By prioritizing support, coaching, and removing obstacles, they create an environment where people can thrive.

A leader who notices when a team member is struggling—not to criticize, but to offer help. They take the time to listen, understand challenges, and then work actively to clear the path ahead. This might mean advocating for resources, simplifying processes, or providing guidance to develop skills. Such leaders do not wait for recognition or credit; their focus is on enabling success for others.

This servant leadership approach fundamentally transforms the traditional top-down leadership model. Instead of a rigid hierarchy where power flows only downward, it becomes a culture of shared ownership and collaboration. People feel seen, valued, and supported, which fuels motivation and loyalty. When leaders serve their teams, they inspire others to serve each other, creating a positive cycle of cooperation.

Ultimately, invisible leaders know that their greatest strength lies not in authority, but in their willingness to serve. This humble, yet powerful approach builds resilient, engaged teams and sustainable success for the entire organization. It is leadership that works quietly but leaves a lasting impact.

4. Listening Over Speaking

Where many leaders dominate conversations, invisible leaders shine at listening. In a world that often rewards the loudest voice, these leaders choose a different path — one of attentive silence and genuine curiosity. They understand that leadership is not about filling every silence but about creating space for others to speak, express ideas, and raise concerns without fear or hesitation.

By truly hearing their teams, invisible leaders unlock a wealth of untapped potential. They listen not just to respond, but to understand deeply what is being said — and what remains unsaid. In that attentive space, hidden issues surface, unseen challenges come to light, and innovative ideas germinate. People feel safe to share their perspectives because they know they will be heard, not judged or interrupted. This kind of listening transforms the dynamic from top-down directives to collaborative problem-solving.

Their silence, far from being a void, is a powerful presence. It signals respect, patience, and trust. In this quiet strength, team members find the confidence to step up, voice their creativity, and take ownership. The leader's restraint invites others to shine and encourages collective wisdom to develop.

Invisible leaders demonstrate that sometimes the most impactful leadership happens in the pauses — in the moments when they listen more and speak less. Their presence speaks volumes, creating an environment where every voice matters and where true innovation and connection can thrive. This is the paradox of invisible leadership: leading by being present in silence.

10.2 The Paradox of Visibility and Influence

This brings us to the paradox at the heart of invisible leadership. We tend to associate leadership with visibility — with being at the front and centre, commanding attention with grand speeches, decisive actions, and unmistakable authority. It is natural to think of leaders as those who stand on stages, whose names light up headlines, or whose presence dominates meetings. But true leadership, the kind that shapes organizations and sustains long-term success, often flows through channels unseen and unheard. Influence—the real currency of leadership—is rarely broadcast with trumpets. Instead, it quietly permeates the everyday actions, the small gestures, and the unnoticed moments that stitch the fabric of culture and connection.

In fact, some of the most impactful leadership occurs in moments so subtle that they escape the spotlight but leave an indelible mark on individuals and teams:

- The manager who remembers an employee's birthday and sends a quiet, heartfelt message of appreciation. No fanfare, no announcement, just a simple, sincere acknowledgment that says, "You matter."
- The team lead who stays late after a tough day, not for praise or recognition, but to help a junior colleague troubleshoot a problem. There's no public credit, no grand statement—only the humble act of support that lifts someone up.
- The executive who chooses to set aside time for a one-on-one conversation to genuinely understand an employee's personal struggles. Instead of a distant company-wide memo about "employee wellness," they create space for empathy and connection that can transform a person's experience.

These moments are invisible precisely because they do not require fanfare or public acclaim. They unfold quietly in hallways, over casual coffee chats, or through a timely message of encouragement. Yet, they build the foundation of loyalty, motivation, and trust that fuels organizational success in ways that no flashy initiative or top-down mandate can replicate.

Consider the power of loyalty born from these silent acts. When a leader takes the time to remember what matters to a team member, it sends a signal far beyond that single interaction: this is a place where you are seen as a whole person, not just a cog in the machine. Motivation grows because people want to contribute to something that respects their individuality and humanity. Trust deepens as employees realize their leaders are not just chasing numbers or outcomes but genuinely care for their well-being and success.

The ripple effects of invisible leadership extend far beyond individual interactions. These quiet gestures build a culture of respect and psychological safety where innovation thrives, collaboration deepens, and resilience strengthens. Employees feel connected not just to their tasks but to a shared purpose nurtured by leaders who lead from behind the scenes.

In essence, invisible leadership reveals that leadership is less about being in the spotlight and more about lighting the way for others—often without recognition or applause. It invites us to rethink how we measure leadership impact, valuing consistency over charisma, presence over position, and service over self-promotion.

For organizations willing to embrace this paradox, the rewards are transformative: a workforce that feels deeply engaged, a culture that sustains through challenges, and leadership that inspires from the inside out. Invisible leadership may not dazzle at first glance, but it builds the invisible infrastructure on which extraordinary success is constructed.

Why the Corporate World Needs Invisible Leaders More Than Ever

Current business environment scenario, the pressure on leaders to be visible, vocal, and constantly "on" has never been greater. Social media, open offices, and digital connectivity mean that leaders are expected to perform—always. The demand for visibility often drives leaders toward superficial or performative behaviours: grandstanding in meetings to grab attention, focusing excessively on optics rather than genuine outcomes, or chasing numbers and metrics at the expense of deeper meaning and purpose. This constant pressure can lead to a leadership style that prioritizes image over impact, spotlight over substance.

But these visible performances come with a steep cost. When leaders focus on being seen rather than being effective, burnout becomes inevitable—not only for the leaders themselves but for their teams. The constant need to "perform" drains energy and authenticity, leading to disengagement and uncertainty among employees. Cultures become fractured as competition for attention overtakes collaboration, and meaningful connections give way to transactional relationships. Their influence grows quietly, through consistent actions that build trust and create psychological safety. They lead with humility, listening carefully, and responding thoughtfully, nurturing resilience not by force but by building genuine connections.

The strength of invisible leadership is in its people-led, values-driven approach. When leaders operate from a place of authenticity, they create environments where individuals feel respected, supported, and empowered. This foundation cultivates sustainable growth because it aligns business success with human well-being, reducing turnover and enhancing loyalty.

Organizations that embrace and cultivate invisible leadership reap powerful benefits, often in unexpected ways:

- Teams feel psychologically safe and trusted. When employees know that their leaders listen without judgment and act with integrity, they are more willing to take risks, speak up, and innovate. This safety is the cornerstone of creativity and continuous improvement.
- Engagement soars, and discretionary effort becomes the norm. People do not just complete tasks—they bring passion and ownership to their work, motivated by a sense of belonging and purpose that invisible leaders adopt to.
- Cultures shift toward collaboration over competition. Instead of jockeying for individual recognition, teams learn to support each other, valuing collective success above personal gain. This mindset fuels synergy and collective intelligence.
- Leadership pipelines develop authenticity over charisma. Future leaders learn that true influence is not about spotlight moments but about steady, genuine presence and service. They are prepared to lead with integrity, empathy, and resilience in a world that demands adaptability and depth.

Challenged with uncertainty, rapid change, and mounting pressures, invisible leadership is not just an alternative style—it is a necessity. It counters the exhausting cycle of performative leadership with a model that centres on what truly matters: human connection, trust, and values. Invisible leaders build not just companies, but communities. They nurture ecosystems where people thrive, innovation flourishes, and organizations endure.

In embracing invisible leadership, we reclaim the true essence of leadership—not as a stage to dominate, but as a responsibility to serve and uplift. This is the leadership our times need and the legacy every organization should aspire to build.

How Can You Cultivate Invisible Leadership?

Becoming an invisible leader is less about acquiring flashy new skills and more about embracing a reflective shift in mindset and daily habits. It is a transformation that moves away from the desire for recognition toward a deep commitment to serve others and the greater purpose. Invisible leadership is not something you turn on or off; it is a way of being—a steady, authentic presence that quietly influences those around you and nurtures a culture of trust, collaboration, and growth.

Here are practical steps you can begin implementing today to cultivate invisible leadership in your life and organization:

Practice humility daily.

Humility is the foundation of invisible leadership. It invites you to pause and reflect: How do my actions serve the collective good rather than just my own ego or ambition? It means recognizing that leadership is not about titles or spotlight moments, but about uplifting others and contributing meaningfully to the whole. Start small—acknowledge the efforts of your team, admit your own mistakes openly, and remind yourself that leadership is a privilege, not a right. This simple shift rewires your mindset from self-centeredness to service, which is the essence of invisible influence.

Listen with intent.

One of the most powerful gifts an invisible leader can offer is truly listening. This goes beyond hearing words—it is about giving your full attention without formulating your response while someone else is speaking. Practice active listening by maintaining eye contact, asking clarifying questions, and resisting the urge to interrupt. This creates space for others to share honestly and have a sense of psychological safety. When people feel heard, they are more engaged, motivated, and willing to contribute their best ideas. Listening is not a passive act but a deliberate strategy for deep connection and understanding.

Serve quietly.

Invisible leaders do not seek applause or public recognition. Instead, they look for ways to support others quietly. This might mean staying late to help a struggling colleague, removing obstacles without making a show of it, or giving credit to others for successes. Serving quietly builds a foundation of trust and loyalty because it communicates that your leadership is genuine and not driven by self-interest. It also models a culture of generosity where everyone feels valued and empowered to do the same.

Be consistent.

Trust is earned through consistency, not grand gestures. Invisible leaders build trust by showing up every day with the same dedication, integrity, and reliability. Small, repeated actions—such as keeping commitments, responding promptly, and treating everyone with respect—send a powerful message: "You can count on me." This steadiness creates a safe environment where teams feel supported regardless of external pressures or challenges. To cultivate consistency, develop daily habits that reinforce your values and leadership principles.

Create psychological safety.

A hallmark of invisible leadership is encouraging a culture where people feel safe to express ideas, admit mistakes, and take risks without fear of judgment or blame. When leaders respond to mistakes with curiosity—seeking to understand rather than punish—they encourage learning and innovation. Promote openness by modelling vulnerability and inviting feedback. Psychological safety is the soil from which creativity, resilience, and engagement grow. It transforms organizations from rigid hierarchies to dynamic learning communities.

Lead by example.

Invisible leadership is less about telling and more about showing. Your behaviours, attitudes, and values set the tone for the entire organization. When you demonstrate empathy, integrity, humility, and accountability, others naturally mirror these qualities. Leading by example creates a powerful ripple effect that influences culture far beyond formal authority. It inspires others to step into their own leadership quietly yet confidently.

This journey toward invisible leadership requires patience and self-reflection. It means questioning traditional notions of power and control and embracing the paradox that sometimes the most effective leaders are those who step back, listen more, and serve first. By shifting your mindset and embedding these habits into your daily life, you become a catalyst—an unseen force driving sustainable success, authentic connection, and lasting impact.

The world often rewards noise and visibility; invisible leadership is a revolutionary act. It challenges us to lead not from the front with megaphones, but from within with quiet strength. And as you embrace this path, you do not just change your leadership style—you transform the very culture of your organization, paving the way for deeper trust, greater collaboration, and a future built on true influence rather than fleeting fame.

The next time you think of leadership, remember Ravi — and countless others like him who shape organizations from the shadows. Recognize the paradox that true leadership is often invisible, yet its effects echo loudly in the hearts and minds of those it touches.

Invisible leadership invites us all to redefine what it means to lead — not as a title or a role, but as a way of being. It challenges us to look beyond the spotlight and honour the quiet forces that truly move the world forward.

10.3 The Essence of Invisible Leadership

Invisible Leadership Begins Within: The Journey to Inner Mastery

Leadership is often pictured as commanding stages, delivering electrifying speeches, or making bold decisions that everyone notices. Yet, there exists a quieter, deeper form of leadership—one that begins not with external actions, but within. Invisible leadership means leading from within first. It is the mastery over oneself—the emotions, thoughts, and ego—that forms the unseen bedrock from which true influence radiates. This leadership style is less about being at the front of the room and more about creating the conditions where others are empowered to shine.

Let me tell you a story about Arjun, a leader who embodied this invisible power. Arjun was a mid-level manager in a large corporation. He never sought the spotlight, rarely spoke in grand meetings, and avoided self-promotion. Yet, his team's performance always exceeded expectations, and his peers respected him deeply. What made Arjun's leadership invisible yet incredibly impactful was his mastery over himself.

Mastery Over Emotions and Thoughts

Arjun understood early on that leadership was not just about strategy or execution; it was about emotional intelligence—the ability to recognize and regulate his own emotions while empathizing with those of others. During a particularly stressful project, when tensions ran high and deadlines loomed, many leaders became reactive, quick to anger or frustration. But Arjun practiced conscious self-awareness. When a team member made a critical mistake, instead of snapping or blaming, Arjun paused. He noticed his rising irritation but chose to respond with calm curiosity: "What can we learn from this?"

His mastery over his emotions created an atmosphere where his team felt safe to admit errors and experiment without fear. This psychological safety was invisible but powerful—it unlocked creativity, collaboration, and resilience. Arjun's steady presence calmed the storm, and his team's confidence grew.

This mastery also extended to his thoughts and ego. Arjun knew his mind often raced with worries about outcomes or doubts about his abilities. But rather than being controlled by these thoughts, he practiced mindfulness—observing them without judgment and gently bringing his focus back to the present moment. This clarity prevented him from making impulsive decisions driven by anxiety or ego.

Creating Space for Others to Shine

True leadership, Arjun knew, was not about stepping forward; it was about stepping back to create space for others to surpass. The invisible leader's power lies in their ability to nurture and empower. This requires immense confidence—not the kind rooted in ego, but in self-awareness and security. When a leader is secure within, they do not feel threatened by others' success; they celebrate it.

Arjun made it his daily mission to notice contributions that others overlooked. He sent quiet notes of appreciation, gave credit generously in meetings, and encouraged quieter voices to be heard. His team blossomed because they felt seen and valued. The culture of recognition and trust became a silent force driving motivation and innovation.

Substance Over Show: The Deep Current of Leadership

Invisible leadership values substance over show, depth over drama, and impact over applause. In a world addicted to visibility, this is a radical choice. Leaders like Arjun demonstrate that the most reflective influence is often invisible. Their power is not in spectacle but in steady, genuine presence.

This kind of leadership requires patience and humility. It means showing up every day with integrity, even when no one is watching. It means making decisions aligned with values rather than popularity. It means cultivating relationships built on trust rather than transactions.

For example, Arjun established weekly "reflection circles" where his team could share challenges and insights openly. These sessions did not have flashy presentations or grand directives. Instead, they offered quiet time to connect, empathize, and realign with shared purpose. Over time, these simple rituals created a healthy, connected team that weathered crises with grace.

Rooted in Self-Awareness and a Higher Purpose

At the core of invisible leadership lies self-awareness—a continuous journey of knowing oneself deeply. It is a commitment to understand not only one's strengths but also blind spots, biases, and fears. Arjun practiced journaling every morning, asking himself questions like, "What attitude will I bring today?" and "How can I serve my team better?"

This daily self-inquiry grounded him and guided his actions. It helped him recognize when ego was creeping in, when stress was distorting his perspective, or when he needed to step back and recharge.

Invisible leaders are also guided by something greater than personal ambition—a purpose that transcends individual success. Arjun viewed his role not just as a manager but as a steward of his team's growth and well-being. This higher calling infused his leadership with meaning and sustained his dedication even in difficult times.

10.4 The Ripple Effect of Invisible Leadership

Invisible leadership may seem subtle or even hidden, but its effects are thoughtful and far-reaching. When a leader master's themselves first, their calm confidence and clarity ripple outwards, transforming teams and organizations.

Arjun's story is an evidence to this truth. His invisible leadership created an environment where people felt safe, valued, and motivated. It nurtured a culture of collaboration and continuous learning, resulting in high performance and lasting impact.

Invisible leadership invites us all to rethink what it means to lead. It challenges the idea that leadership is about visibility, control, or loud authority. Instead, it asks us to start within—to master our emotions, thoughts, and ego—and to lead with humility, presence, and service.

As you progress on your own journey of invisible leadership, remember this: The most powerful influence is often the one you cannot see, but always feel. When you lead from within, you become the key catalyst that shapes not only corporate success but the human spirit within your organization.

Small Acts, Massive Ripples

Leading Without Spotlight: The Power of Small Acts in Invisible Leadership

Leadership is often thought of as a grand scene. We picture bold statements from a stage, comprehensive visions announced with dramatic feel, or heroic moments that capture everyone's attention. Yet, the truth is far more nuanced. Invisible leaders do not wait for these grand moments to lead. They lead quietly, steadily, through small, consistent acts — acts that may seem ordinary on the surface but carry extraordinary power underneath.

Let me introduce you to Kavita, a team lead in a large technology firm. Kavita was not known for bombastic speeches or headline-making decisions. She did not seek accolades or dominate meetings. But anyone who worked with her knew that her leadership was a subtle force that held the team together and propelled them forward.

Small Acts That Build Big Trust

Kavita understood the value of a sincere "thank you" — not a generic, passing comment, but a personalized acknowledgment that recognized specific effort. When Rahul, a quiet programmer, stayed late to fix a tricky bug, Kavita sent him a thoughtful message the next morning, thanking him by name and highlighting how his dedication saved the team from a potential delay. Rahul felt seen, valued, and motivated to continue giving his best.

This was no accident. Kavita made it a habit to notice efforts others overlooked — the person who quietly cleaned up a shared workspace, the junior colleague who volunteered to help with tedious data entry, or the team member who offered a fresh idea in a brainstorming session but quickly retreated to the background. She believed that recognizing these small contributions promoted psychological safety — the sense that people mattered, their work mattered, and their voice mattered.

Psychological safety is the invisible glue that holds teams together. It allows people to take risks, share honest feedback, and innovate without fear. Leaders like Kavita create this safety not through grand pronouncements but through repeated, small acts of acknowledgment and care. This consistency weaves a fabric of trust that strengthens every interaction and decision.

The Ripple Effect of Quiet Influence

Influence is not measured by volume but by value. A quiet word of support can change the trajectory of a person's career. Consider Ramesh, a junior analyst who struggled with confidence. During a tough project phase, Kavita took a few minutes to quietly mentor him, helping him break down complex tasks and reassuring him that mistakes were part of learning. She did not make a show of it — no public praise, no spotlight — but this quiet investment empowered Ramesh to grow and contribute meaningfully.

Likewise, invisible leaders often perform unseen efforts to remove barriers that slow their teams down. For Kavita, this meant quietly negotiating resources with other departments, smoothing out conflicts, or clarifying confusing instructions. She did not announce these behind-the-scenes interventions, but they saved projects from derailment and reduced frustration within the team.

These small acts accumulate like drops in a reservoir, filling it with trust, loyalty, and motivation. The team may not always see the source of this strength, but they feel its impact every day.

Leading Through Rituals, Not Rhetoric

Kavita also understood the power of rituals — simple, recurring practices that reinforce shared values and culture. She did not believe in flashy team-building exercises or forced enthusiasm.

Instead, she established small, consistent rituals that aligned with her leadership philosophy.

Every Friday afternoon, she held a five-minute "shout-out" session where team members could express gratitude for one another's help during the week. This ritual was informal and low-key but powerful. It cultivated a habit of appreciation and shifted the team's focus from individual achievements to collective effort.

In another instance, Kavita started the practice of beginning meetings with a brief moment of reflection or a positive story from the week. This small pause created space for mindfulness and connection, reducing stress and developing empathy. Again, no grandstanding, just a steady nurturing of the culture.

Why Small Acts Matter More Than We Think

Why do these small acts carry such weight? Because leadership influence is fundamentally relational. It is about the quality of connections between people. Big gestures may catch attention but often do not sustain relationships. Small, consistent acts build emotional deposits that nurture trust and loyalty over time.

Research in organizational psychology shows that people remember how they are made to feel more than what is said or done in grand moments. A leader who remembers your name, notices your effort, or listens when you speak sends a powerful message: "You matter." This message is the currency of commitment.

Invisible leaders embrace this reality. They focus on being present and attentive in these everyday moments. Their influence flows quietly through the network of relationships, shaping culture and performance without fanfare.

The Paradox of Visible Impact from Invisible Acts

If a boat is sailing across a sea. The captain steering the ship may be visible to the crew, but under the surface, countless currents, unseen by the naked eye, guide and stabilize the vessel. Invisible leaders are those steady currents — stabilizing, directing, and powering the journey in ways that do not seek attention but demand respect.

This paradox invites us to reconsider what leadership looks like. It challenges the myth that leadership must be loud, extroverted, or charismatic. Instead, it highlights the power of humility, patience, and authenticity.

Action Insights: Lead with Small Acts

How can you cultivate this invisible leadership style through small acts? Here are some actionable steps that anyone can practice daily:

- **Thank People by Name, Sincerely and Specifically:** Do not settle for generic "thank you." Take a moment to identify exactly what the person did and express your appreciation with genuine warmth. This small effort makes your recognition memorable.
- **Notice and Appreciate Efforts Others Overlook:** Develop a habit of observing the subtle contributions in your team. It might be someone who quietly supports others, solves a problem without asking for credit, or always shows up with positive energy. Pointing these out builds morale.

- **Make Time to Mentor or Coach Quietly:** Leadership is about developing others. Even brief moments spent coaching or mentoring can have long-lasting effects. Offer your support without expecting public recognition.
- **Build Rituals that Reinforce Values Without Fanfare:** Create simple routines or traditions that reflect your team's culture and values. It could be a weekly appreciation round, a moment of gratitude at meetings, or a shared practice of mindfulness. These rituals embed leadership into everyday life.

Your Leadership Legacy

As you reflect on your own leadership journey, consider this: What small act of leadership will you commit to today? How will you invest in invisible influence that nurtures trust and empowerment?

Leadership is not a title or a moment in the spotlight. It is the sum of the small, consistent actions that ripple through your team and organization. Invisible leaders may not be the loudest in the room, but their legacy is the strongest — carried in the hearts, minds, and successes of those they serve.

Lead quietly, lead consistently, and lead with purpose. The world needs more invisible leaders like Kavita—leaders who show us that sometimes the softest voice echoes the loudest in the halls of success.

The Calm Catalyst Truth #10:

"The Power of Presence — Leading Beyond Words"

CHAPTER 11

THE SPARK UNNOTICED: BEING "THE CALM CATALYST"

11.1 Trust: The Silent Backbone of Invisible Leadership

Among the leadership qualities, trust stands tall as the silent, unshakable backbone. It is the invisible thread that weaves individuals into cohesive teams, ideas into successful ventures, and moments into legacies. Without trust, even the most charismatic, loud, or authoritative leaders falter. They may command attention temporarily, but their influence is fragile, prone to collapse when tested.

Invisible leaders understand this deeply. They know that trust is not a given — it must be cultivated patiently, regularly, and authentically. Unlike flashy gestures or loud proclamations, trust is earned silently. It speaks not in volumes but in the quiet certainty with which people believe in their leader's intentions, character, and actions.

The Paradox of Trust in Leadership

Trust is paradoxical in many ways. It is both fragile and resilient, invisible yet powerful, earned slowly but lost quickly. Many leaders mistakenly believe trust can be bought with perks, titles, or speeches. The truth is far different: trust is built in the mundane, everyday actions that reveal who you truly are.

Anil, a midlevel manager in a multinational company. Anil's leadership style was quiet but steady. He was not the loudest voice in meetings, nor the most flamboyant decision-maker. But his team trusted him implicitly. Why?

Because Anil showed up every day as the same dependable person. When he promised support, he delivered. When he made a mistake — which he did, like anyone — he admitted it openly and worked to fix it without excuses. He communicated transparently, sharing information honestly even when the news was difficult. Above all, Anil treated every team member with dignity and respect, making each person feel valued beyond their job title.

This consistent pattern of behaviour built a reservoir of trust that made his leadership invisible but deeply felt.

Consistency: The Pillar of Trust

One of the cornerstones of trust is consistency. Trust is fragile when actions are unpredictable or contradictory. Invisible leaders build trust through reliable, repeatable actions — the kind that make others feel safe and secure.

Consistency means doing what you say you will do, every time. It means honouring commitments, whether big or small. It means showing up emotionally and mentally present, not just physically.

Consider Maya, the CEO of a fast-growing startup. Her team admired her not for grand strategic announcements but for her unwavering commitment to integrity. She never promised what she could not deliver, and when external factors caused delays or changes, she communicated honestly and promptly. Even in crisis, Maya's calm and consistent presence grounded her team.

This dependability created a culture where people knew they could count on leadership. They felt confident to take risks and innovate because the foundation of trust was solid.

Transparency: The Bridge to Trust

Transparency is another essential ingredient. Invisible leaders understand that trust thrives in the light, not in shadows. They communicate openly and honestly, sharing relevant information with their teams, even when the message is tough.

Transparency is not about oversharing or divulging every detail. It is about being truthful and timely in communication. It means resisting the urge to spin or sugar-coat realities. It means inviting dialogue and feedback rather than issuing top-down directives.

Rajesh, a senior leader in a manufacturing company, was known for his candid style. When the company faced layoffs, Rajesh did not hide behind corporate jargon or delays. He convened meetings to explain the situation plainly, answered hard questions, and expressed empathy for affected employees. This openness did not remove the pain but helped preserve trust.

Employees trusted Rajesh because he treated them as adults, worthy of truth, even when it was uncomfortable. Transparency created a shared understanding and aligned everyone's efforts toward recovery.

Authenticity: The Heart of Trust

Trust cannot be faked. Invisible leaders build trust by being authentic — true to themselves and consistent in their values. Authenticity means showing vulnerability, admitting mistakes, and acknowledging limits without fear of judgment.

An authentic leader does not pretend to have all the answers or be perfect. Instead, they demonstrate humility and courage by being honest about challenges and seeking help when needed.

Take the example of Sita, a non-profit director. She openly shared her learning journey with her team — her missteps, doubts, and growth. This vulnerability encouraged others to do the same, promoting a culture of psychological safety.

Authenticity invites connection. When people see the real person behind the leader's role, trust blossoms naturally. It humanizes leadership and breaks down barriers.

Keeping Promises and Admitting Mistakes: Trust Builders in Action

Trust is built as much in admitting failures as in keeping promises. Invisible leaders understand this well. They honour their word and do not overpromise. When they err, they own the mistake promptly and transparently, focusing on lessons learned and corrective action.

This behaviour counters a common leadership pitfall — the fear of appearing weak or flawed. Instead, invisible leaders recognize that admitting mistakes is a strength, not a weakness. It models accountability and builds a learning culture.

Consider Arun, a project manager. When a project under his leadership failed to meet deadlines, Arun convened a candid review session. He acknowledged his role in the delays, invited feedback without defensiveness, and collaborated on solutions. His team respected him more for this honesty than they would have for a defensive cover-up.

Prioritizing Dignity: The Foundation of Trust in Every Interaction

Every interaction, no matter how small, carries the potential to build or erode trust. Invisible leaders prioritize the dignity of every person they engage with. They treat others with respect, kindness, and fairness, recognizing the human behind every role.

This focus on dignity means listening fully, refraining from judgment, and honouring commitments to others' well-being. It means recognizing the intrinsic value of everyone, beyond their output or status.

Leela, a department head, made it her practice to greet every team member personally each morning. She asked about their well-being and genuinely listened. This simple act conveyed respect and care, reinforcing a culture of mutual trust and belonging.

Action Insights: Build Trust Daily

Building trust is not a one-time event but a daily practice. Here are practical steps to embed trust-building into your leadership routine:

- Follow Through on Commitments, No Matter How Small
- Communicate Openly and Honestly
- Admit Errors Openly, Focusing on Learning and Growth
- Prioritize People's Dignity in Every Interaction

The Long-Term Power of Trust in Invisible Leadership

Trust built through invisible leadership is durable and transformative. It creates an environment where people bring their best selves to work, collaborate openly, and innovate fearlessly. It transforms organizations from mere places of transaction into communities of purpose.

Invisible leaders may not seek headlines, but their legacy is profound: teams that thrive, cultures that endure, and results that speak louder than any speech.

Empowerment Over Control

Invisible Leadership: Empowering Others, Not Controlling Them

Leadership, as traditionally assumed, often invokes images of command and control — the leader at the helm, steering the ship, making all the decisions, and directing every action. This old paradigm focuses on authority, hierarchy, and top-down mandates. But the truth about truly effective leadership, especially in an active and complex world, is quite different. Invisible leadership flips the script: it is not about controlling others but about empowering them.

Invisible leaders understand that their power is not measured by how much they direct or dominate, but by how much they enable others to lead themselves. They create conditions where autonomy flourishes, initiative is encouraged, and individual growth is nurtured. These leaders celebrate the successes of others as if they were their own because they know that empowering others multiplies impact far beyond what any one individual can achieve.

The Shift from Control to Empowerment

The urge to control is natural. Leaders often feel the pressure to ensure outcomes, manage risks, and meet deadlines, which can lead to micromanagement. But micromanagement affects creativity, dampens motivation, and undermines trust. Invisible leaders consciously resist this impulse and choose a different path: they create space — physical, psychological, and emotional — for others to step into their power.

This shift requires humility and confidence. It is a paradox: you must be secure enough in your own role to let go of control and trust others to take charge. It demands patience, allowing room for mistakes and learning. But the rewards are tremendous — teams that are engaged, innovative, and resilient.

Encouraging Initiative and Risk-Taking

Invisible leaders encourage initiative. They do not wait for perfect conditions or explicit permission to act. Instead, they make an environment where team members feel safe to take risks, try new approaches, and learn from failures.

This empowerment requires a culture that embraces learning over blame. Raj, an operations leader, once shared a story about his team experimenting with a new process to reduce turnaround times. The experiment initially failed, causing delays. But instead of reprimanding the team, Raj held a review session focused on what could be learned. The team analysed what went wrong, adapted their approach, and succeeded on the second attempt.

Raj's willingness to encourage initiative and accept failure without judgment inspired his team to push boundaries and deliver continuous improvements.

Supporting Growth and Development

Invisible leadership also means prioritizing the growth of others. These leaders are deeply invested in the development of their team members' skills, confidence, and careers.

Supporting growth involves personalized attention. Invisible leaders recognize individual strengths and aspirations, then align roles and projects to maximize potential. They act as mentors and coaches, providing guidance without micromanaging, asking thoughtful questions, and challenging people to stretch beyond their comfort zones.

Consider the story of Aisha, a team leader in a consulting firm. She took the time to understand her team members' unique capabilities and career goals. For one member with strong analytical skills but limited client exposure, she assigned tasks that required client interaction, offering support along the way. For another who was hesitant to speak up in meetings, she encouraged small contributions and celebrated those moments publicly.

Aisha's team thrived under her empowering leadership. They gained new skills, increased confidence, and felt genuinely supported.

Celebrating Others' Successes as Their Own

True empowerment means relinquishing the need for credit and recognition. Invisible leaders celebrate the successes of their teams wholeheartedly. They understand that leadership impact is multiplied when others shine.

When Ravi, a department head, publicly acknowledged a junior employee's innovative idea that saved a major client contract, the ripple effect was insightful. The employee felt seen and motivated, colleagues were inspired to contribute more actively, and Ravi's team culture shifted towards greater collaboration.

Celebrating others' achievements strengthens relationships and reinforces trust. It signals that leadership is a collective effort, not a solo act.

Empower Your Team

To cultivate invisible leadership through empowerment, leaders can take the following practical steps:

- Delegate With Trust, Not Fear
- Encourage Experimentation and Learning from Failures
- Recognize Individual Strengths and Align Roles
- Create Forums for Team Voices to Be Heard and Valued

11.2 Humility: The Silent Power Behind Invisible Leadership

When we think of leadership, images of boldness, decisiveness, and confidence often come to mind. These qualities are celebrated and sought after. Yet, every truly effective leader lies a quieter, often overlooked strength: humility. Humility is not weakness or timidity; it is the silent power that fuels invisible leadership.

Humility means having the courage to step back, to admit you do not have all the answers, and to share credit generously. It is about embracing vulnerability without fear, being open to learning, and recognizing that leadership is not a solo act but a collective journey. This silent power of humility creates an environment where innovation thrives, collaboration deepens, and people feel safe to bring their whole selves to work.

The Courage to Step Back and Admit You Don't Know

Humility begins with honesty — honesty with oneself and others. It takes courage to admit that you do not have all the answers. Many leaders feel pressured to project certainty and control, fearing that admitting uncertainty might undermine their authority or respect. But the invisible leader knows otherwise.

Take the story of Anil, a senior executive at a large manufacturing company. During a strategic planning meeting, Anil was faced with a complex challenge no one had a clear solution. Instead of pretending to have the answers, he openly acknowledged the unknown and invited ideas from the team.

This moment of humility shifted the energy in the room. People felt valued and empowered to contribute, sparking a collaborative problem-solving process. Anil's willingness to be vulnerable did not diminish his leadership; it enhanced it. He built trust and encouraged a culture of learning.

Humility requires emotional strength. It means acknowledging limitations and using them as an opportunity to engage others, not to retreat.

Encouraging Openness and Learning

Humility opens the door to continuous learning. Invisible leaders do not see themselves as the final authority; instead, they remain curious, open to innovative ideas, and willing to be challenged.

This openness creates a culture where mistakes are seen as learning opportunities rather than failures to be punished. It encourages experimentation and innovation because people feel safe to voice their thoughts and try innovative approaches.

Ramesh, a team leader in a software company, demonstrated this beautifully. After a major software release encountered unexpected issues, instead of blaming the team, he gathered everyone to reflect on what could be improved. He openly shared his own mistakes during the process and encouraged the team to do the same.

This humble approach strengthened the team's resilience and sparked a continuous improvement mindset that boosted future product quality.

Humility fuels psychological safety — the foundation of learning and innovation.

Building Connection Through Humility

Invisible leadership is deeply relational. Humility helps leaders connect authentically with others, bridging gaps of hierarchy and status.

By being approachable and acknowledging shared humanity, humble leaders encourage trust and rapport. They listen with empathy, validate feelings, and create a space where people feel comfortable being themselves.

For example, Anjali, a director in a non-profit, made it a habit to check in regularly with her staff, asking not just about work but about how they were coping personally. She openly shared her own challenges, creating a culture of mutual support and understanding.

This genuine connection boosted engagement and well-being across her team, proving that humility is as much about heart as it is about mind.

Humility deepens human connection, making leadership more effective and humane.

The Silent Strength That Creates Safe Spaces for Innovation

Innovation requires risk-taking and the freedom to experiment. But that freedom depends on psychological safety — the feeling that one won't be punished or ridiculed for taking risks or making mistakes.

Humility in leadership creates these safe spaces. When leaders admit they do not have all the answers and accept imperfection, it encourages others to do the same. It breaks down the fear of failure and opens creative potential.

Consider the case of Dev, a startup founder who regularly shared his learning failures with his team, from product flaws to marketing missteps. His transparency made the team comfortable sharing their own setbacks and brainstorming solutions without fear.

This culture of humble openness was critical to their ability to pivot quickly and innovate in a competitive market.

Humility lowers defensive walls and sparks collective creativity.

Practical Examples of Humble Leadership in Action

Let's deepen the understanding of humility with real-world examples:

The Manager Who Listens More Than Talks:

Suresh, a middle manager, was known for his quiet demeanour but relentless listening. He asked open-ended questions and encouraged his team to express concerns and ideas fully before sharing his views. This humility made his team feel valued and often led to innovative solutions that Suresh might not have conceived alone.

The Leader Who Admits Mistakes Publicly:

Priya, a senior executive, publicly acknowledged a strategic misstep during an all-hands meeting. She described what went wrong, what she learned, and how the company would adapt. This act of humble transparency increased trust and reduced fear of failure across the organization.

The CEO Who Shares Credit at Every Opportunity:

Rajesh always deferred praise to his leadership team and frontline employees. During a product launch celebration, he said, "This success belongs to every hand and mind that contributed — thank you for making this possible." His humility united the company and inspired loyalty.

Is Humility Your Leadership Strength?

To deepen your own humility, reflect on these questions:

- When was the last time I openly admitted a mistake or limitation?
- How often do I ask for feedback and act on it?
- Do I celebrate the successes of others more than my own?

- How comfortable am I with silence, listening, and not having all the answers?
- In what ways can I practice humility in my daily leadership interactions?

Ultimately, humility is the heart of invisible leadership — the quiet force that propels teams and organizations toward enduring success.

11.3 Leading Beyond Titles and Positions

Invisible Leaders Rise above Hierarchy: Leading from Wherever You Are

In traditional views of leadership, influence is often equated with formal authority and positional power. The leader stands at the top of an organizational chart, issues directives, and commands attention by virtue of their rank. But invisible leadership challenges this outdated paradigm. It teaches us that true leadership is not confined to titles, corner offices, or hierarchical status. Instead, it resides in the quality of presence, the strength of relationships, and a mindset grounded in integrity and purpose.

Invisible leaders transcend hierarchy. They lead wherever they are — in a cubicle, on the frontline, in a team meeting, or during informal conversations in the hallway. Their influence is not granted by position but earned through actions that add value, build trust, and inspire others. This form of leadership is subtle yet powerful. It is accessible to anyone willing to step up with intention, regardless of their place on the org chart.

The Myth of Positional Power and Its Limitations

Hierarchical leadership assumes that influence flows downward from the top. While formal authority can facilitate decision-making, relying solely on position limits the reach and impact of leadership.

People may follow out of obligation, not commitment. This can breed disengagement, resistance, and transactional relationships. The rigid hierarchies often suffocate creativity and slow down responsiveness in a fast-paced, complex business environment.

Invisible leadership offers a more dynamic model, emphasizing personal agency and relational influence over title-based control. It recognizes that leadership happens through networks, conversations, and shared purpose — not just formal commands.

Quality of Presence: The Essence of Invisible Leadership

One of the key attributes of invisible leaders is their quality of presence. Presence is more than physical attendance; it is about being fully engaged, aware, and authentic in interactions.

For example, Kavita, who does not hold a managerial title but always brings a calming and focused presence to stressful meetings. She listens carefully, asks pointed questions, and offers thoughtful suggestions without seeking the spotlight. Her calm confidence reassures colleagues and subtly guides conversations toward productive outcomes.

Kavita's leadership is invisible in the sense that it does not shout or command but gently influences through steady presence and credibility. Her colleagues naturally gravitate toward her input because she adds real value.

This example shows that leadership influence can arise from being "present" — mentally, emotionally, and ethically — no matter your formal role.

Strength of Relationships: The True Value of Influence

Invisible leaders understand that leadership is relational. The strength of their influence depends on the trust, respect, and goodwill they build with others.

Arjun, a mid-level analyst in a multinational firm, makes it a priority to develop authentic relationships across departments. He regularly checks in with peers, offers help on cross-functional projects, and shows genuine interest in others' work and challenges.

When a critical project needed coordination between marketing and finance, Arjun's network and rapport enabled smooth collaboration. His influence extended well beyond his job description because people trusted and valued him.

Leadership that transcends hierarchy thrives on this network of relationships. Invisible leaders act as connectors and facilitators who break down silos and help collaboration across boundaries.

Influence Is a Choice: Stepping Up with Integrity and Purpose

One of the most empowering truths of invisible leadership is that influence is a choice — not a privilege reserved for the titled few.

Anyone can choose to lead by stepping up with integrity and purpose in their daily work.

This means:

- Taking initiative without waiting for permission.
- Speaking up with courage and respect when something matters.
- Supporting colleagues and amplifying diverse voices.
- Aligning actions with personal and organizational values.

For instance, Priya, a customer service representative, noticed recurring issues in customer feedback but saw no formal process to address them. Rather than waiting for her manager's direction, she took the initiative to compile data, propose solutions, and collaborate with product teams to improve service. Her proactive leadership improved customer satisfaction and earned her recognition beyond her job title.

Stepping up as an invisible leader requires inner conviction and ethical grounding. It is about serving a purpose greater than oneself.

Lead from Wherever You Are

Invisible leadership can be cultivated through intentional daily habits. Here are some practical steps:

1. Identify Opportunities to Add Value Beyond Your Role
2. Build Bond Across Teams and Functions
3. Stay Curious About Others' Perspectives and Challenges
4. Champion Causes That Align with Organizational Values

Real-World Examples of Leading Beyond Hierarchy

To explain invisible leadership transcending hierarchy, consider these stories:

- The Administrative Assistant Who Leads Culture:
  Anita, an executive assistant, supported a culture of gratitude and inclusivity by organizing informal celebrations, recognizing milestones, and welcoming new hires. Her positive influence created a cohesive and motivated work environment.
- The Junior Engineer Who Advocates for Diversity:
  Sameer, a junior engineer, noticed a lack of diversity in hiring. He researched best practices, engaged HR, and helped launch an inclusion task force. His advocacy improved hiring policies, even without a formal title.

Cultivating a Leadership Mindset at Every Level

Invisible leaders transcend hierarchy by cultivating a mindset that:

- Sees leadership as a responsibility, not a reward.
- Values contribution over control.
- Embraces continuous learning and growth.
- Prioritizes relationships over transactions.
- This mindset creates a sense of ownership and accountability regardless of rank.

The Organizational Benefits of Invisible Leadership

Organizations that embrace invisible leadership at all levels experience:

- Greater agility through distributed leadership.

- Enhanced collaboration and knowledge sharing.
- Higher employee engagement and empowerment.
- Stronger alignment with values and purpose.

This creates resilient cultures that thrive in complexity.

11.4 Being "The Calm Catalyst"

Today, the world demands endlessly for attention, recognition, and speed. The idea of invisible leadership stands as a quiet yet thoughtful revolution. Whether in business, politics, or everyday life, is fixated on visibility. We measure success by how loudly one can speak, how many followers one commands, or how quickly results appear on spreadsheets. The noise is deafening. But invisible leadership invites us to pause and reconsider: What if the most reflective influence comes not from the loudest voice or the fastest move, but from a steady presence, humble service, and consistent integrity?

Invisible leadership asks something radical and deeply human of each of us. It calls us to lead not by demand or authority, but by example. It reminds us that leadership is not merely the power to give orders or the spotlight to be grabbed, but the quiet power of deeds done well, of kindness extended without expectation, and of empathy practiced when no one is watching. It is a call to move away from ego-driven actions toward those inspired by genuine care and commitment to others.

What makes invisible leadership so powerful—and so accessible—is that it does not rely on formal titles, large teams, or grand stages. It requires none of the traditional markers of "leadership" that so many chase. Instead, it invites every individual to step forward in their own capacity. Whether you are a frontline employee, a mid-level manager, or a seasoned executive, the core elements are the same: a commitment to inner growth, the courage to serve quietly, and the consistency to build trust over time.

Inner growth is foundational. Invisible leaders understand that true influence begins within. It means cultivating self-awareness—recognizing your emotions, biases, and triggers—and choosing how to respond with intention rather than reaction. It means developing emotional resilience to remain calm and clear amidst uncertainty and chaos. This inner mastery allows the invisible leader to create a stable presence that others can rely on—a beacon of steadiness in a turbulent sea.

Courage is equally essential, but not the kind that roars from a podium. It is the quiet courage to serve without applause, to admit mistakes openly, and to put the needs of others before personal glory. This courage transforms vulnerability into strength, and openness into connection. It is the bravery of a leader who asks for feedback, listens with humility, and adapts to serve the greater good.

Consistency is the glue that binds invisible leadership together. It is not about grand gestures that flash and fade, but the daily, often unseen acts of reliability—following through on commitments, acknowledging others sincerely, creating safe spaces for honest conversations, and nurturing growth in those around you. Over time, these small actions build a foundation of trust so solid that it can weather storms and inspire loyalty that lasts.

As you close this book, I invite you to embrace the role of the invisible catalyst in your world. Your leadership does not have to make headlines to make a difference. It can be felt in the calm you bring amid chaos, in the silent support you offer when no one is watching, and in the empowerment you advance quietly through trust and encouragement.

Think about the ripple effect if more of us chose this path—organizations where psychological safety is the norm, where people bring their whole selves to work, where collaboration replaces competition, and where every individual feels seen and valued. This is the transformative power of invisible leadership. It changes cultures, improves performance, and most importantly, nurtures human dignity and connection.

Your leadership can transform your organization, your community, and even your family—not by being seen, but by being deeply felt. This is the true essence of leadership: the power you wield when no one is watching, the impact you create in the spaces between words, and the legacy you leave through the lives you touch.

Step into your invisible power with confidence and grace. Lead with humility, serve with empathy, and build with unwavering consistency. The world needs more leaders who understand that sometimes the loudest voice is silence—and the greatest strength is quiet influence.

Invisible leadership is not just a style or a strategy; it is a way of being. It is leadership that respects the human spirit, uplifts those around us, and ultimately, creates a world where leadership is no longer a privilege of the few, but a possibility for all.

The Calm Catalyst Truth #11:

"Leadership That Listens, Lifts, and Lasts"

CONCLUSION

Win From Within – The Silent Revolution Has Begun

Success is not an accident. Excellence is not a coincidence. And culture? It is never a committee-driven slogan written on a wall. Culture is what happens when no one is looking. Leadership is who you are when the spotlight is off. That is the truth this book has attempted to awaken in you.

Through every chapter, every story, and every insight, one message has echoed loud and clear: **Real change starts within. The Calm Catalysts do not make noise, they make an impact.**

Today, more than ever, we do not need louder leaders. We need deeper ones. We need organizations that do not just grow but grow in soul. We do not just need high performance; we need high purpose. And here's the best news: You have everything you need to build that right now.

You may be a manager, an analyst, a vice president, or even an intern. Your title is not your power. Your awareness is. Your integrity is. Your energy is. When you begin to align with your values, with your truth, and with your inner boardroom, you become unstoppable.

Just think about it: The best strategies fail in toxic cultures. The sharpest minds get dulled in energy-draining environments. But even the simplest ideas thrive in organizations where people feel seen, valued, and safe.

Every culture is built either by design or by default. If you do not shape it, it shapes you. And what is the blueprint of a thriving culture?

- It is emotional energy that flows cleanly.
- It is rituals that create rhythm and respect.
- It is leaders who listen with presence, not just position.
- It is systems that remove friction and fuel collaboration.
- It is the invisible that fuels the visible.

Let this book be your compass. But **YOU!! must take the steps.**

From Knowing to Doing: Actionable Wins

You now know the silent powers. So, what's next? Let's move from intention to action.

- **Start noticing.** Every day, observe your team's energy. Is there lightness or heaviness? Is there trust or tension? Learn to sense what is not spoken.
- **Ask better questions.** Not just "What are your goals?" but "What do you need to succeed?"
- **Recognize the invisible.** Appreciate people for effort, for care, for things that do not show up on dashboards but change lives.
- **Hold space, not just meetings.** Create environments where people can speak without fear. Lead conversations where they feel heard, not just reviewed.

- **Lead your inner boardroom daily.** Reflect. Recentre. Align. Remember, the most critical conversations are not the ones in the boardroom, but the ones in your heart.

These are not small changes. These are seed changes. Plant them constantly, and you'll watch a forest of excellence grow.

Your organization is waiting

Your organization is not a logo or a building. It is a living, breathing ecosystem of emotions, values, energies, and hopes. It is shaped by every small decision, every hallway conversation, and every unspoken message.

If you are reading this, it means you are ready. Ready to lead the silent revolution. Ready to be the force that creates cultures of courage, clarity, and compassion. Ready to walk the talk, quietly but powerfully.

The world changes not by chance, but by choice and today, the most important choice is yours.

"You bring the energy. You create the clarity. You build the culture. You are the Unspoken Calm Catalyst."

A Thoughtful Disclaimer

As this book draws to a close, I want to pause and speak not just as an author, but as a fellow traveller in the world of corporate leadership—a world where ambitions are high, timelines are sharp, and the pressure to deliver is persistent. If you have read this far, you have likely resonated with the nuances, stories, and subtle forces described in *The Calm Catalyst.* You've probably seen shadows of your own leadership journey reflected in its pages. But before you return to your meeting rooms, your brainstorms, and your dashboards, a humble disclaimer—a perspective meant not to reduce the ideas in this book, but to properly situate them.

The Calm Catalyst is not a framework, formula, or fix-all. It is not a rejection of traditional business obligations, nor a criticism of results-driven leadership. This book is a point of view—a lens through which to re-examine what often remains invisible in our daily chase of goals. The dynamics explored here—emotional energy, unconscious patterns, presence, and universal culture—are not *alternatives* to performance. They are the *undercurrents* that often determine whether performance is sustainable, meaningful, and People-led.

This Is Not a Rebellion Against Results

Let me be clear: Results matter. Targets matter. Margins matter. Strategic execution and operational excellence are foundational pillars of any successful business. No amount of emotional intelligence, cultural alignment, or silent leadership can substitute for the raw discipline required to execute, deliver, and outperform. This book does not argue otherwise. Instead, it suggests that amidst those necessary disciplines, there are *quiet forces*—forces that, if left unacknowledged, can erode even the most knowledgeable strategies. To put it simply, this book is not an escape from performance pressure; it is an anchor within it.

This Is Not a Prescription, But an Invitation

Every leader's journey is unique. The environments we operate in vary vastly—from high-growth startups to global enterprises, from mission-driven nonprofits to hard-nosed turnaround projects. What works in one culture may seem alien in another. So, the insights shared here are not blueprints. They are invitations. You may find some chapters resonate deeply with your context. Others may challenge your current beliefs. That's the intent.

You are encouraged to take from this book what aligns with your journey and leave the rest without guilt or defensiveness. Leadership is an evolving art, not a checklist. There is no one-size-fits-all when it comes to emotional resonance, psychological safety, or cultural patterns. This book simply seeks to bring awareness to things that are often felt but rarely named.

Leadership Has Many Languages

Some leaders inspire through action. Others through vision. Some by being the loudest voice in the room. Others through their calmest presence. There is room for all these styles. *The Calm Catalyst* does not suggest that quiet leadership is superior. It merely reminds us that *quiet* is not *absence*. That stillness is not indifference. That sometimes the most powerful leaders are the ones who create space, not noise.

In a world that glorifies visibility, this book celebrates *substance.*

In a culture obsessed with charisma, it honours *credibility.*

In times of transactional urgency, it gently turns our perspective to *transformational presence.*

Respect for the System and Its Pressures

Let me also acknowledge that many leaders—perhaps you included—operate under extreme constraints. Investor expectations, shareholder demands, Leadership vision and goals, cost pressures, workforce volatility, market unpredictability… none of these disappear when we start speaking about empathy or energy. And this book does not intend to ignore or underestimate those realities.

Rather, it seeks to offer you tools to endure and evolve amidst those pressures. Not by resisting them, but by resourcing yourself. Emotional intelligence is not a luxury. Energetic presence is not fluff. Cultural clarity is not a soft skill. These are strategic enablers—especially in high-stakes environments where burnout, attrition, and disengagement quietly bleed potential.

This book is not here to replace your business toolkit. It is here to enhance it.

A Tribute, not a Disruption

In many ways, this book is a tribute. A tribute to all those silent leaders who never chased the spotlight but always lifted others. To the managers who asked how their team was *really* doing. To the engineers who saw patterns in chaos. To the HR professionals who sensed cultural drift before anyone named it. To the CXOs who knew that business success is not just what you build, but how people feel while building it.

It is also a tribute to the leadership legacy that shaped me—especially to visionaries like Vineet Nayar, whose *Employees First* philosophy deeply impacted my foundational beliefs. His work didn't undermine performance—it made it personal, humane, and participatory. I hope this book, in its own voice, carries forward that lineage—honouring the invisible threads that hold people, purpose, and performance together.

Interpret With Curiosity, Not Finality

Lastly, let me ask that you interpret the ideas in this book with curiosity, not finality. Don't turn it into another rulebook or checklist. Let it be a living dialogue—within yourself, with your teams, across your cultures. Use it to question, to reflect, to recalibrate. Let it sit beside the spreadsheets, the roadmaps, the quarterly business reviews—not as a contradiction, but as a quiet companion.

- Where strategy draws the map, let presence light the path.
- Where execution drives the engine, let emotional energy fuel the journey.
- Where structure defines the skeleton, let culture animate the soul.

You are the best judge of what your context needs. You know your people, your pressures, and your possibilities. This book simply asks you to look at all of it—*again*, and differently. The catalysts it describes may be unspoken, but they are significant. If they whisper to you, listen. If they stir something in your leadership approach, explore. And if they remind you that leadership can be both high-performing and deeply human, then they have served their purpose.

Because at the heart of it all, performance that is not connected is often not sustained.

> *Thank you for walking this journey with me—quietly, curiously, courageously.*
>
> **— Brahmanand Savanth**

"The Calm Catalysts: How Silent Leaders Drive Bold Wins" is not just a book. It is your blueprint. Your mirror. Your call to rise.

ACKNOWLEDGEMENTS

This book is the result of countless invisible pushes, silent inspirations, and the solid support of people who believed in me—even before I fully believed in myself.

First and foremost, I offer my deepest gratitude to my family. Your patience, love, and understanding during the long hours of writing and reflection gave me the strength to keep going. Every page of this book carries your silent sacrifices and unspoken encouragement from you.

To my mentors, leaders, colleagues, and teams across the years—you may not realize how your everyday actions, challenges, and insights shaped this book. A special thank you to those quiet leaders—The Calm Catalysts—who showed me the power of presence over position, integrity over influence, and consistency over charisma. You are the Pulse of this book. A special word of thanks to Vineet Nayar, whose book *Employees First, Customers Second,* planted an early seed in my mind about reimagining leadership from the inside out.

To my readers, current and future—thank you for your curiosity, your search for meaning, and your belief that leadership is not always loud. I wrote this for you.

Finally, this book wouldn't exist without Some Divine Blessing (The SDB); some journeys are not walked alone, even when no one seems to be around. For that invisible company, I remain forever thankful.

— *Brahmanand Savanth*